SHE'S ALL OVER THE PLACE

By
Erica "Ms. Precious" McGee

Copyright © 2021 by Erica "Ms. Precious" McGee

All rights reserved. No part of this book may be reproduced or transmitted in any form or by any means without written permission from the author.

All scriptures are taken from the King James Version of the Bible unless otherwise stated.

ISBN: 978-0-578-35047-9

Paperback

Printed in the USA

TABLE OF CONTENTS

Foreword 1
Acknowledgments 5
Vocabulary 9
Introduction 26
Chapter 1 - Who am I? 33
Chapter 2 - The Cow and the Rhino at the Waffle House .. 51
Chapter 3 - The Green Jolly Rancher 59
Chapter 4 - 5am Flashlight 63
Chapter 5 - Get off the panic button 69
Chapter 6 - The Lady on the Billboard 77
Chapter 7 - The Day Before 31 85
Chapter 8 - Do You Do Leadership Training? 91
Chapter 9 - Can we go to Lunch? 100
Chapter 10 - The Laundry Room 105
Final Thoughts 113
Conclusion 116

FOREWORD

You're always at the right place at the right time; at least that's what I believe. I was told by my virtual assistant/project manager, at the time, whom I called "Kim Possible" that I had a gift of asking the right question to the right people at the right time. I guess it's true because as you read you will find that every mentor I ever had started with me asking a simple question. I sat on the front row of the Atlanta Barber Conference and boldly raised my hand and asked Steve Harvey's retired barber, James "JT" Thomas, to lunch in a conference room full of people. Here are his thoughts below:

I had just finished speaking at the Atlanta Barber Conference April 2019, telling my story of how I became Steve Harvey's personal barber of thirty plus years. I talked about my career in the TV industry, not only as a barber but as a road manager, movie producer and almost anything behind the scenes you can think of in the industry. You know all the stuff behind the scenes that no one sees, but without it, it wouldn't be possible. As always, I allotted time for questions after, I had spoken many times before and received many questions but this particular young lady not only stood out but she stood up and asked a question no one has ever asked and I was intrigued. No one had ever asked me that question before and I honestly wanted to know why.

SHE'S ALL OVER THE PLACE

She boldly stood up in a room full of people with pink, orange, and yellow hair and asked me if we could go to lunch. At the time I didn't know what to think! But I knew I couldn't go to lunch because I had a flight to catch. But that didn't stop me from wondering what she wanted to go to lunch for. After explaining I had a flight to catch, she responded I can come to Texas. I smiled and closed out the session, took pictures and returned to the DFW where my barber college is located.

Erica reached out to my assistant at the time and inquired about attending my barber college. I followed up with an email and we set a time to talk. Once I talked to Erica, I was very interested in what she had to say. She said she admired who I was and the things I had done and that she really wanted to learn from me and that she needed to know what she needed to do to make that happen. I told her I had a school down in Fort Worth, TX and she said she was going to come. I didn't really think she was going to come because people say that all the time and then I never hear from them anymore but this young lady was consistent, persistent and very determined. I told her I would be in Atlanta for Steve's Mentoring camp and she asked if I had enough volunteers to cut hair and if she could attend. I invited her and that gave me a chance to find out a little bit more about who she was as a person. A month later she relocated to Texas as she said she would and we had lunch early July in Arlington, TX at Olive Garden near the Dallas Cowboys stadium. As we ate lunch, I remember her smiling and saying I told you I was coming to Texas to have lunch with you!

If I had to describe Erica in one word, I would say she is ambitious. She goes for what she wants and if she tells you she is going to do something she does it either on time or

Foreword

before time. Most people don't do what they say they're going to do but Erica does and I like that about her. I saw that in her and that's why I use her as my assistant. She has helped me with several projects. She has great qualities and I enjoy working with her. She shared with me that it was one of my barber instructors Ms. ShaRon Gaut who gave her a call one Saturday morning and said you're getting ready to write your book and it's going to be called "She's all over the place" and you're going to tell the world what that means to you. She told me that she had been told that she was all over the place for years, so she decided to turn that into a positive and she said that going forward when people told her she was all over the place it just meant that she was going to be international someday. I told her that's all over the place if you're international that's everywhere. I'm so proud of how far she has come and I know her future is bright.

This book is full of personal development and leadership lessons she has learned throughout her career and experiences as a young stylist and entrepreneur. Her eagerness to continue learning and sharing is extraordinary and I believe that's what it takes to succeed. When you take extra and ordinary and put them together you get extraordinary, and this young lady has what it takes to go all the way.

James "JT" Thomas

ACKNOWLEDGMENTS

I would like to take a moment to thank God for not only waking me each morning and giving me more grace than I deserve but for giving me the desires of my heart so that he could give me the desires of my heart. Sometimes it doesn't even seem real. I have to pinch myself to make sure I'm awake. I'm blessed beyond measure and for that I am thankful. I want to thank my parents, my biological father, Lonnie Davis, you passed away when I was 8 months old however your blood still runs through my veins and I love you (rest in heaven daddy). My mother Linda McGee- Henderson my twin well I guess I'm your twin because all my life I have been told "you look just like your momma", thank you for making sure I had a relationship with my creator. My daddy John Henderson (step father) you have been there since I was one years old. There is a lot to say about a man that will take care of a child that is not his own. Thank you for always being my cheerleader and believing in my dreams no matter how big or small. To all my brothers, sisters, nieces, nephews, godchildren, grandparents, aunts, uncles and cousins I love and appreciate your support know matter how big or small I love and appreciate you.

To all my best friends I had beloved y'all! I have the infamous title as being the "professional best friend maker." Thank you for all the phone calls, can you send me some money calls, can I sleep in your spare bedroom or on your living room floor calls, all the prayer calls and so much more I am forever thankful for all fiftyleven of yall, you know who you are!

To my pastor, therapist and mentors without you I wouldn't be the woman, mentor, leader, friend and entrepreneur that I am today. I'm forever grateful.

To all my clients past, present, and future I appreciate your business and I thank you for not only allowing me to comb your hair, print for you or service you in some type of way. Thank you for allowing me to leave a footprint on your life. I thank you for allowing me to love you and your children as my own family not to just provide a product or a service.

To my person, my love, my partner, my heartbeat in human form, my homie lover friend, you get me you support me be it with a listening ear, financially or with a simple smile I love and appreciate you. We actually like each other!

There are so many people that have impacted my life over the years too many to name, but I want you to know that I appreciate everything that has ever been done or said for me because it all has played a role in my success as a person and as an entrepreneur.

Last but not least I wanna thank Me! I want to thank me for being all over the place and accepting it! I wanna thank me for always putting God first. I wanna thank me for overcoming every obstacle set in my way, I wanna thank me for being brave enough to believe in me when no one else did. I wanna thank me for always being a giver and never quitting. I wanna thank me for moving forward even when I was broke, broken and homeless, and it looked like I had nowhere to turn. I wanna thank me for trusting the process for not only crying through it but for growing through it ok y'all go ahead and read this good book it might even change your life!

Before we get into this thing let's talk about your verbiage, your vocabulary, because that's some really important stuff. Especially if you want to win at this thing called life!

VOCABULARY

Vocabulary Words for Life as an Entrepreneur

Please keep in mind these are my definitions. Not all will be found in the Webster dictionary or interpreted the same. These are my personal opinions, none of these definitions have been googled; they are all from my experiences as an entrepreneur. However, I would like you to google these words for a better understanding if you feel the need to do so and find the true definition for yourself.

You may proceed...

A.C.T. (Acceptance, Commitment, Therapy) - What I underwent to learn how to process my past traumas, heal and move forward.

Adulthood - A trap (I'm just playing...no I'm not); the responsibility to handle your business in all aspects of life once you enter what some would call the real world.

Assistant - The person you hire to keep you on track and to run those errands that you don't have time to run because you are doing IPA (Income Producing Activities).

Associate - Someone you have connected with on a mid-level.

Author - Me! LOL seriously though, the person who decides to and accomplishes the goal of putting words to paper to share their thoughts and views on a subject matter, publishes the work and shares it with the world. The creator of your own life written, spoken or lived.

Average - Doing the minimum.

Best Friend - The person you call that is there for you no matter what. Your biggest cheerleader and supporter. I have 7 of these and they all serve a different purpose in my life.

Bio - The document that describes who you are, what you do and what's in it for the person reading it. It's what everyone wants to know when they meet you.

Break - Something you take before you drown in despair. It's ok to take a break; a moment to rest and realign yourself with your core values.

Business owner - The person that starts the business with the mindset that their company will run itself if they are there or not because they started with a business plan.

Business plan - The recipe for your company contains who your business is, your mission, what you do and your objectives and what's in it for your target market, your financials, the budget and start-up cost to bring the business to life. Don't let it overwhelm you; it could be one page if that is what it takes to get you started.

Business poor - Putting more into your business than you receive. Your business is a source of income. It's not a person or an emotion as money does not have emotions and it doesn't care who possesses it, however, it will do whatever you assign it to because your money is an employee, a soldier in your army and it's up to you to decide how you put it to work.

Calculated Risk - It's when you come up with a game plan, discuss it with your team and weigh all your pros and cons and make an educated decision on your next move.

Cashflow - Money to operate your business and your life.

Certifications - Something you seek out in order to have access to funds available for minorities, women, veterans, LGBTQ and so much more. It is important to get your certifications to take your business to the next level.

Chamber of Commerce - Where you go to get connected in your city with other businesses.

Champion - You, yes, you reading/ listening to this right now because you are winning. The person who sees it through no matter how tough it gets!

Character - The type of person you are; you do the right thing even when no one is looking.

Cheerleader - People that root you on when you are working towards bringing your dreams to fruition or reality.

Coach - A person or persons that help lead, guide and train you to greatness.

Complaining – What you do when you're ungrateful. Take a moment to realize how blessed you are.

Compound Interest - The 8th wonder of the world; the effects of small habitual behavior or habits over a period of time. This is why the Tortoise always wins the race. Slow and steady.

Consistency - Repetition, the thing you must do over and over and over and over and over and over and over and over again in order to get the results that you desire and deserve.

Consultant - Someone you hire to assess where you are and where you are going. Your consultant should be in your field and aids in the success of individuals or businesses helping to make decisions based on their knowledge in that field.

Contagious - A winning attitude. People love to be around positive people and you will often hear them say it's contagious because it spreads.

Corporation - Very high business filing that requires a board and could yield better tax breaks/advantages. A filing that takes place once your business reaches a certain income bracket.

Credit/Credit Cards – What you must have in order to use OPM (see definition of OPM). Only use up to 30% of your credit limit and pay down to zero balance monthly.

Delayed Gratification - How you build a sustainable level of success. She took her time and came up with a game plan and she waited and didn't rush the process.

Delegate - What leaders learn to do in order to grow their business because they know they can't do it alone.

Depression - What you fall into when you don't get out of your feelings. It's ok; you may end up here for a while and that's ok because it may very well be a part of your journey. Just don't stay there. Get present in your moment and seek therapy, meds, friends or whatever it takes to leave that state of mind because depression is a state of mind.

Destination - A set place you are going. My destination is Hawaii. Life, however, is not a destination; it's a journey.

Discipline - The thing you must have in order to attain any and every goal you have and it ranks up there with oxygen.

Dominate - To take over; she dominated her industry and took no prisoners (sometimes you have to use that thing in a sentence).

Dream - The thing that keeps you up at night; the thing you can't stop thinking about until you do what it takes to bring it to life!

Elevator pitch - Who you are, what you do and what's in it for the person you are talking to in 30 seconds or less.

Employee - The person you hire and pay to help run your business. The person that is not vested in the company because they are only paid for the task they do and know they can be replaced at any time.

Energy - Something you must protect at all times.

Entitled - People expecting something for nothing.

Entrepreneur - The person who starts a business the person who takes a step of faith and starts the business not knowing what's going to happen.

Extra - Doing what I like to call the most! Going above and beyond what everyone else does; making a bold statement and setting the standard for excellence.

Failure - To attempt something and not succeed which is the true way to success. If you never attempt, how will you accomplish what you set out to do? It's a no brainer; fail your way to success, I did!

Faith - The substance of things hoped for and the evidence of things unseen aka that stuff you have to have to survive.

Family - The people in your life that will be there for a lifetime not just a season. They could be blood relatives or non-blood people.

Feelings - Something you must stay out of; they can be dangerous.

Financially Challenged - Some would refer to this as being broke however it just means your funds are currently low.

Forgiveness - That thing they say that's for you and not the person that did you dirty. It's for YOU. Forgive yourself for not living up to those high standards that you set for yourself.

Friend - Someone familiar that shares common interests, you enjoy being around and that supports you.

Future - The moment you're preparing for; it's not promised to you so use your time wisely.

Goals - The things you set daily, weekly, monthly, yearly that you wish to accomplish.

Grace - What God gives us daily and what we don't give ourselves enough of; be kind to yourself.

Vocabulary

Growing Pains - The part of your journey that elevates you to the next level; this part hurts because you are shedding your old skin breaking those muscles down so they will grow bigger and stronger.

G.T.S. (Google That Stuff) – Utilize the internet when you don't know what something is; just utilize your resources. Google will be your friend.

Gym - The place you go to relieve stress and to protect your temple. Your body is your temple and you only get one so take care of it daily.

H. O. T. S. (Hare, Owl, Tortoise, and the Squirrel) - Your team's characteristics. They all have the characteristics to make a great fully functional team. Ask yourself which is your strength and which is your weakness.

Habits - The things you do unconsciously without any thought. It's like second nature to you. Creating good habits once you have identified the bad habits that do not serve you will be a game changer in the long run.

Haters - What you will have no matter how much you do or don't do, so just do you and be great. People can't do things themselves so they speak ill of those who make things happen.

Healing - The thing that you must accept and do before you can really step into your greatness.

Homelessness - Your name is not on a lease or deed. You live in your car, on your friend's couch or in your momma's basement, but not necessarily on the street. So, in other words, if your name isn't on a lease, legally you are homeless and you can google that one.

Hopelessness - A feeling of despair and defeat. A feeling almost everyone experiences in their life time at some point.

Housekeeper - Someone you should hire to help with time management once you achieve a certain status in your business and in life.

Humility - The person that can take a compliment without bragging or boasting. Something you will either learn the hard way or the easy way.

Integrity - Doing what you say you're going to do; honoring your word.

Insanity - Doing the same thing over and over expecting different results.

Instant Gratification - microwave success that doesn't last. Example- It's my success and I want it now!

I.F.S. (Internal Family Systems) – A form of therapy that explains how to heal and acknowledge the different parts of yourself.

Investor - The person that earns money with their money.

I.P.A. (Income Producing Activities) - The things you do daily to produce cash flow in your business.

J.O.B. (Jesus Ordained Blessing) - This will keep you Just Over Broke if you let it, however, it will allow you to build the capital to start your own business and of course pay your bills.

Journey - Your life is a journey, a whole experience. It will lead you to many places based on the decisions you make on a daily basis.

Kill Joy - Sometimes known as the voice of reason or the person always shooting down your dreams. Also known as a dream killer. This person has many names but is very valuable to you because, as a visionary or leader, sometimes you lack the ability to see what could go wrong so you need these people on your team.

Leader(ship) - A person that guides, trains and develops a group of people with a common goal. He/she leads from the front and is the example for the team. He/she allows the team to drive the ship but never gets off the ship.

Lesson - What you learn from every situation in life. You either learn what to do or what not to do; either way, you learn.

Life insurance - Income replacement so that in the event your life is taken unexpectantly, your family can still receive your income every month. It's not just money to bury your loved ones. It should be enough to cover the death, income, mortgage and education needs for the family. Again, it's more than just money for a funeral. Planning while you are young is the key to securing generational wealth.

Life - What you are living every single day. The question is, "What kind of life do you want to live?"

Line of credit - Monies extended to you from a bank or credit union that is somewhat of an open loan.

LLC (Limited Liability Company) - This is a business filing that protects your personal assets from your business assets.

Love - Something you do unconditionally.

Marketing - The look of your company and what you do to grow it. This is one of my favorite things because it comes natural to me.

M.B.A. (Massive Bank Account) - Something everyone wants but most won't work for because they think it's too hard. If it was easy, everyone would do it. Hard work pays off and one of the rewards is a massive bank account.

Mental Health - The state of your mind, asking yourself daily or recognizing your state of mind. Mental health is vital to accomplishing day to day tasks. Your mental health can be good, bad, healthy, or unhealthy. It's up to you to assess your mental health daily and recognize your triggers.

Mentors - Those who came before you, paved the way and have reached back or allotted time and resources to help others not make the same mistakes. Someone you can learn from.

Mindfulness - Being aware of your mental state at all times and being present in the moment. Most people are either thinking about the past or the future and you have no control over either.

Mission - You find this in your business plan and this should contain your core values. The things you stand on and the reason you do what you do.

VOCABULARY

Money - A tool to afford your life's experiences. Some only want to experience paying bills and maybe taking a trip while others desire luxury vacations and going on holiday for a month at a time.

Motivation - It's like taking a bath; you have to do it every day sometimes 3 to 4 times a day to keep yourself going.

Mouth - Something you should pray and ask God to help you keep closed. You have to know when to be seen and when to be heard.

Objectives - What you set out to accomplish.

O.P.M. (Other People's Money) - Sometimes it takes this to build and grow a business.

Opportunity - Closed mouths don't get fed and if you don't have an option available to you, create one. It's also the thing you take or create to take you to the next level and make your dreams a reality.

P.U.S.H. (Pray Until Something Happens) - That's what my mother always told me to do.

Pain - What you go through sometimes. That thing that hurts, however, sometimes it's just what you need to change.

Past – Yesteryear. Yes, I said yesteryear. It's over, it's gone, you can't change it, you appreciate it and learn from it but you don't relish in it except to heal from it and move forward.

Patience – What you have deep inside of you already; you just have to exercise it. The more you ask for patience, which is the ability to deal with things without going off the deep end, the more situations you will get to prove your patience, so just thank yourself for being patient and take your time.

Personal Development - A skill developed to work on one's self and become better at whatever it is you do.

P.H.D. (Public High School Diploma) - Something almost everyone has and something so many people don't use. You have everything it takes to be successful.

P.R.T. (Public Relations Team) - A group of persons that help get you in front of who you need to be in front of in the media.

Present – This very moment; the most important moment because what you do now affects your future self.

Priority - Things you should do first because it's most important.

Procrastinate - Something you do when you're all over the place and you're avoiding your responsibilities. Something you may think is a bad thing but it could be the universe lining up that exact moment you are supposed to cross paths with someone.

Project Manager - The person you hire to organize your thoughts and bring clarity to each project you desire to work on so there is no confusion. They make the impossible possible for the creative geniuses of the world.

Provision - What will be provided for your vision to come to fruition.

Prune Juice - The stuff you drink so you can let that ish go! It stinks and you have sat in it long enough and it's now time to process, heal and move on. You have lives to change, but first you must change your own, so let it go.

Rejection - Something you must learn early on to deal with and not take personally.

Relationships - Something you must cherish, build and make deposits in regularly with those that you love.

Rest - Something you must do to allow your body and mind time to regenerate so you can continue to go out and be great on a daily basis. It's life's medicine and we can't produce without it so take care to rest regularly.

Results – What you get once you put the work in. Without the work, you cannot have the results and the end game is not possible unless you put the work in.

Retirement - The accumulation of enough funds that you can live off the interest of that money. Starting young gives you a great advantage. Plan to save $500 a month, which is $6k a year. That is if you want to retire with seven figures and live off the interest.

Retreat - Something you must take or go on to recoup your losses if you have run into hard times or just to relax or rejuvenate.

Reward - What you get when you win after you have put in all the hard work that it takes to accomplish your goals.

R.O.I. (Return on Investment) - The thing you calculate when making a decision to invest in something or someone.

Rule of 72 – Divide 72 into any number to find out how long it takes to double that number.

S Corp - Business filing that you use once you are earning at a higher income level.

Sacrifice - What it takes to win; giving up today for what you will have tomorrow.

Savings - Money that will save you if you save it. 3-6 months of your income should be the savings goal. I heard that my whole life and it took a pandemic for me to realize the severity of accomplishing this goal.

SCORE (Service Corps of Retired Executives) - Free business coaching in your local city and state. Check your local listings to find out more information about your local SCORE organization. It changed my career.

Self-Care - Time dedicated to appreciating yourself.

Self-Control - What you must exercise in order to go to the next level. Taking control of your emotions and responding instead of reacting.

Self-Employed -The person that works **in** their business more than they work **on** their business. The person that decides to go after their dreams and works for themselves.

Serenity - That thing that grants you peace and the ability to accept the things that you can't change and the wisdom to know the difference. Some call this the serenity prayer.

Skin in the Game - Experience and time learning your craft; you have gone from talking about it to being about it.

S.M.A.R.T. (Specific Measurable Attainable Realistic Time Frame) – When setting goals, you want to use this system. It will aid in the attainment of your goals.

Vocabulary

Social Media - A tool that will allow you to reach people around the world, A way to connect, build and grow a business from your home or anywhere in the world if used wisely.

Sole Proprietor - Lowest level of business filing for one individual and is taxed at a higher rate.

Someday/One Day – Days that are not on the calendar, so do it today!

Speaker - What you become once you have a story to tell worth listening to that can add value to the listener's life.

Stop - What you have to do sometimes so that you can regroup but please try not to stop for too long.

Story - What you listen to and learn from others that have gone before you. Also, what you share with the world once you have become a true overcomer.

Strength - Something you don't realize you have until you have to use it; what it takes to pull through the hard times.

Success - The completion of a worthy ideal no matter how big or small. If you say I want to be a barber and you become a barber, you are a success. If you always say nothing when people ask you what's going on or what are you thinking and you never have anything going on then you are successful at nothing. Read that again. Nothing doesn't exist. Think twice; speak and do once; your words are powerful.

Sweat Equity - What you have to put in to receive a return on your investment. Sometimes you will have to give your products or services away for free. Also known as skin in the game. You better go get you some. Read that last line again for clarity!

Taxes – Money you pay to the IRS monthly or quarterly on the money you earn. Typically, 8-15% (consult your accountant).

Team - The people you will delegate tasks to in order to run a successful company because you cannot do it all on your own. Trust me you will get tired; I know from experience.

Tears - The water that comes from your eyes when you're happy and sometimes when you're sad; either way, let it flow. You always feel better after a good cry.

Temptation - The thing you resist in order to accomplish said goal or task.

The Tithe - The first 10% of whatever you earn that you give back to your creator. Whether it be to your church, a charity, or a random stranger who may be struggling. I have literally given my stash $100 bill to a guy on the side of the road who said he was starting a new job but needed help to buy clothes and food for his family.

Time – Your most valuable asset. It's one of those things you can't get back so I advise you to use it wisely.

Travel - What you do to get away from it all. I heard that all work and no play is simply not what it is. So let's take a vacation and not a trip! Spend the money on the nice room and luxury rental car and experience all that life has to offer, within reason, or not; it's up to you to create the life you desire to live.

Venting – What you do when you're full and need to get it all out. Please be sure to announce that you are venting, not to be confused with complaining, there is a difference. You have to vent to the right people.

Vision - The big picture. The idea or vision you see yourself turning into a reality. The thing that sometimes no one else will see but you. The thing you must hold on to at all times and only share with other visionaries.

Wisdom - What you have after you have been through a few things and you have learned your lesson.

Working Smart - Means taking calculated risks and not just jumping in headfirst. Doing research or hiring someone to do research so you don't continue to make the same mistakes.

I hope you liked all these good vocabulary words for life! It's important to renew your mind daily. Listening to motivational videos, audio books, scriptures and more are important along your journey to self-discovery. Remember motivation is like taking a bath: you have to do it daily!

> *And be not conformed to this world: but be ye transformed by the renewing of your mind, that ye may prove what is that good, and acceptable, and perfect, will of God. Romans 12:2*

INTRODUCTION

Before we get started, I would like to congratulate you on being in a space of clarity and focus in this season of your business and your life. Repeat after me out loud so your inner self can hear you; all those parts of yourself that are ALL OVER THE PLACE! Yes, I need all those parts to hear you and listen. Are you ready? Ok, here we go. Repeat after me:

I am amazing, great, and a genius!

I am even brilliant, powerful and happy!

I am successful!

I have the best day ever Every day!

I love you and I mean it!!!!

Ok! let's get started shuga!

I learned that in life when you get old, people will listen to you. They will even sit around and listen to you tell stories because you have lived your life and you have wisdom to share. But when you're young, you better have a story to tell and it better be a good story. I can honestly say I have more stories than I care to share. But there are a few stories and lessons that impacted my life and my hope is to share them with you and that they will impact your life, business, or future business in a positive way. Life has taught me so many lessons, lessons of leadership, personal and professional development, humility and so much more. I learned it's not about you; everything you're going through is not about you. A Pastor said this and it felt like he said it only to me even though I was sitting in a sanctuary full of people. Go forward knowing that in the rough times that it's not about you; it's about pushing through to the other side so you too can share your story. It may change or save someone's life.

How I Journal

So, for years now I have done this thing where I document the day of the week, date and time that I write things down so I decided to incorporate that here. We all have little weird quirky things that we do that makes us who we are and some would say they are significant and others would say otherwise. I say, go for what you know and do what makes you happy.

The 9-year-old

July 22nd

2:50am

Thursday

As I sit at my newly put together dining room table and chairs from Ikea at almost 3am I would like to share a few stories that changed my life. Let me tell you about the 9-year-old.

"Ms. Precious"

"Yes Madison"

"I don't feel like getting my hair done."

"Madison"

"Yes Ms. Precious"

"I don't feel like doing your hair!"

I had been doing Madison's hair since she was about 4 years old and I believe we had a pretty good relationship. But we were not feeling it on that particular day. By this time, I had my own salon on Covenant Rd. in Columbia, SC. It was previously a dentist office and I decided to use what was probably the dentist's office because it had its own private bathroom and built-in bookshelf. My workstation faced the street with a big bay window. We had a small parking lot, which fit about 4 or 5 cars. As I continued to do Madison's hair, we continued our conversation about how neither of us was thrilled about today's appointment. I told Madison if I don't do your hair then I won't make any (comma pause for effect) MONEY! As I said the word "money," a $1 bill was floating by in the parking lot. I yelled for Madison to run outside and catch it before it floated away. She did as I instructed and retrieved the $1 bill and when she came back in, I traded the dollar bill for 4 quarters. In all fairness, she did do the work. I said just like that dollar bill was floating by, if I don't work, then I won't earn any money.

We continued our quest to style Madison's hair and it was quiet for a while when Madison said, "Ms. Precious?" Yes Madison. She paused for a second and said, "Wouldn't it be cool if we could earn money in our sleep?" All I could do was shake my head, look up and smile. About a week prior I had just attended a 3-day conference teaching exactly that: how to earn money in your sleep and I had told any and every one that I came in contact with how to do it and they all looked at me like I was a crazy person. It was easy. All you do is buy something of value and then you rent it out. But it was like talking to a brick wall! So, I decided to just keep my big mouth shut about it and that was that.

Madison wasn't having it; she was only 9 years old, but she wanted to know how because I answered her and told her she could earn money in her sleep. After she begged me to tell her, I explained what some would call the cashflow quadrant.

There are only 4 ways to legally earn money in America. You're either an Employee, Self Employed, Business Owner, or Investor. After a quick explanation, Madison quickly decided she wanted to be a business owner and investor seeing as the goal was to earn money in her sleep. Now I had to explain to this nine-year-old how to purchase, own and operate a business. The average person would say why even bother she's only 9 years old? Good thing I'm not average.

So here goes.

Let's say you saved your allowance for a year, all your birthday and Christmas money and you ended up having $2500. That's a lot of money, right? Yes, ma'am, Madison said. I replied that's not a lot of money Madison. But let's say it's enough to go buy a used ice cream truck. The look on her face was priceless. I said now hold on, you have two choices. You can either ride around in the ice cream truck all day and try, key word is try, which means to attempt to sell ice cream or you can rent the truck out to someone else and charge them to ride around all day and try to sell ice cream. Whether they sell any ice cream or not they still have to pay you rent.

She pondered on the thought for a moment and said, "I want to rent it out."

I said OK now do you want to get paid every week, every other week, or once a month? She excitedly said every week.

I asked her how much she wanted to charge them. After a short silence her response was "$100 a week sounds good Ms. Precious." I said OK well there are 52 weeks in a year so you will earn $5200 and the initial investment was $2500 so your ROI is more than what you initially invested. You earned the money you spent on the truck and another $2700. How does that sound? "Good!" she excitedly responded. So now you're going to do it again duplicating the process.

Before that day, when I performed hair services on kids, we played the quiet game if you can get my drift. It was my first lady from Bethel AME church who told me her key to staying young was working with children. So going forward I decided to put more into my hair babies and I even started a mentorship program called the Beautiful Me Dream Team because if you have a team, you can accomplish your dreams and every dream needs a team. You can't do it alone.

There is a lesson in every story I share. That day the "9-year-old" helped me discover my love for working with children as well as you can teach anyone anything no matter their age if they desire to learn.

The next story I will share is called "The Nail."

"It don't hurt bad enough," he said.

In life we change for one or two reasons. We either change for pain or for pleasure.

INTRODUCTION

Every day a young man walked to work as he passed by this man's house; he noticed his dog was sitting on the porch moaning. He said to himself if the dog is moaning tomorrow when I walk by, I'm going to ask why his dog is moaning? Sure enough, the next day like clockwork the dog was moaning. "Excuse me sir, may I ask why your dog is moaning? Oh, he's just sitting on a nail. Well, why won't he get up?

It don't hurt bad enough, he said."

You're probably sitting on a nail right now; maybe two or three. Your venting has turned into complaining and you just can't understand how you got in this predicament in the first place. News flash! The answer is You yes You! You got yourself there and you will get yourself out! Just hold on and keep reading.

I listened to this story countless times from one of the greatest motivational speakers of all times, Les Brown. I have also shared this story with clients and countless people I have encountered in an attempt to help them get off the nails in their life and begin the healing process so they can move forward. Just like I want you to move forward if you're currently stuck on the nails of life.

This story helped me to get off one of my biggest nails which was the struggle with my weight. The struggle was real and I was tired of being fat. I weighed over 270lbs in my mid 20's, but I was cute. I even did a survey that said would you date the cute chunky girl or the ugly girl with a nice body? Everyone said the cute chunky girl so for a long time I didn't care about being fat well overweight. But it wasn't until my best friend's 25th birthday which led up to my 25th birthday just a few months later that I couldn't take it anymore. My thighs rubbed together so bad I had to walk up my stairs with my legs gapped apart so they wouldn't touch because they stung and burned so badly from chaffing. I'm pretty sure I cried that night and I made the decision to start my weight loss journey and get off that nail known as obesity and take responsibility for my actions. I lost 100 pounds in 2015. After a few years life happened and I experienced depression with a side of anxiety and gained the weight back and then some. I jokingly say I played lost and found with 100lbs. My highest recorded weight being 297lbs like my friend said, I was a few french fries and cookies, cakes and brownies away from being 300lbs. And I'm too short to be that big! I'm proud to say that I have since healed from the depression and anxiety with the help of my awesome creator, my therapist and my tribe and I am currently shedding the pounds and preparing for my first body transformation/ fitness competition show this fall in October.

No matter what you go through, always remember these words: "This too shall pass."

Chapter 1

WHO AM I?
WHAT I DO?
WHAT'S IN IT FOR YOU?

Ask yourself: How do you walk into a room?

Are you the person whose confidence walks in the room first and introduces you by your aura?

Can you read the room to see if the person that you're looking to connect with is present?

August 30th

11:41pm

Monday

Who you are, what you do, what's in it for me?

When you meet someone for the first time, whether you know it or not, you want to know these three things.

Who they are, what they do, and what's in it for me or how can we benefit from each other?

So here goes...

Who am I?

- Child of God
- Humbly Confident
- New to the DFW Metroplex (I relocated on the 4th of July from Columbia, SC)
- I'm a serial entrepreneur since the age of 21 years old that loves all things business and marketing
- College dropout (did one year at Benedict college in Columbia, SC. My major was business and marketing)
- Licensed Cosmetologist and barber
- Owner of Beautiful Me Hair Studio
- Owner of BME Screen Printing, a marketing firm (the company I grew too fast)
- Founder of M3: "The Motivate Me Movement"
- Six figure income earner for several years (I grew my businesses too fast without a solid infrastructure and became overwhelmed and fight or flight kicked in and I took a 5-year flight)
- Developer of two mentorship programs: "The Beautiful Me Dream Team" salon mentorship / marketing team and "The BME Ambassadors" screen print shop mentoring / marketing team. I worked with several local colleges, The Richland County sheriff's department Youth Arbitration Program as a community service site. I offered young adults both male and female peer mentoring and service-learning hours as well as internships unpaid and paid.

What I do
- I comb hair, motivate, inspire and encourage people to follow their dreams!!!!
- C: I care for hair
- O: I'm optimistic
- M: I'm a natural motivator
- B: I'm going to bring out the "Beautiful Me" in you!
- M3: I literally gave my little sister some free motivation to encourage her to speak life and claim the job she applied for after she graduated from college and she said that's right sister "motivate me!" The motivate me movement was born!
- Very simply put I created a design that allows you to put almost anything over motivate(s) me and on the back of the shirt there is a whole list of affirmations known as "free motivation"
- I'm a consultant, speaker and author

What's in it for my clients, potential clients and readers?
- My hair clients - receive professional hair care services. Ranging from cutting, color, braids, relaxers, extensions and more. I even offer scalp analysis with a microscope magnifying the scalp up to 400x just to name a few. I am also a multi-cultural stylist servicing male and female clients of all races.
- I specialize in healthy hair which is what most clients are striving for from a stylist and barber.
- The client receives relaxing head and hand massages with service at no additional charge.
- BME Screen Printing/M3 clients receive professional printing services. Easy to order systems for full functionality. M3 is a fundraiser project created to benefit schools, teachers, students and their families.

- My reader will gain knowledge and know-how from my experiences and many lessons as a young budding entrepreneur.

If someone asked you to write down who you are would you know what to write?

At first, I thought you would say of course but when I put people on the spot and play the icebreaker game I created known as Who am I? they often draw a blank as to who they are and say out loud to themselves "Who am I?"

There is a lesson to be learned at all times. I learned that in life people want to know who you are, what you do and what's in it for them. Are you even worth knowing? Sounds kind of harsh but you unconsciously feel the same way about the people you meet and you should. You want to know who I am and why I'm all over the place and what that really means. You probably already know that the struggle is real! Leadership, growth and development never ends.

So, who am I you ask? Why should you read or listen to the rest of this book? I'm so glad you asked because it's time for my favorite icebreaker. You can use this one if you like, it's on the house and it's actually fun. I turned it into a game. I literally play it with my clients while I do their hair and have for years. Seeing that I'm all over the place I like to have fun so here goes.

First thing you have to do is grab a piece of paper, create a T chart and on the left side you will write I Am and on the right side you will write I Am Not. Then you set a 3-minute timer and fill each side with who you are and who you are not. It's the coolest thing ever, especially with kids! I usually put people on the spot. That's what makes me who I am and what makes the game so fun. In being true to who I am, I am telling Alexa to set a three-minute timer right now. I'm about to play the game now and continue to let you know who I am then I will tell you what I do and what's in it for you!

After the timer goes off you must stop writing and count how many you have on each side, write it down and circle it. Here goes!!!

Who am I?

I AM	I AM NOT
Love	Broke
Peace	Fat
Author	Lazy
Sister	Mean
Friend	Bossy
Humble	Depressed
World Traveler	Anxious
On TV	Poor
On Radio	Homeless
Hair Stylist	Fearful
Billionaire	Hopeless
Child of God	Struggling
Happy	Self-Destructive
In Love	Overspending
Helping People	
Grace	14
On a weight loss journey	
Aunt	
Wife	
Mother	
Barber	
Personal Assistant	
Photographer	
Published	
Debt Free	
Visiting Africa	
26	

Whew, that was fun! And a little bit challenging as I am usually doing this with paper and pen and not on the computer, but I made it and boy does three minutes go by fast. As you can gather by reading this some of my I Am's are actual current facts and some are my goals, dreams and aspirations. Guess I could have put a big dreamer on the I am side. But the fun part is you can play this game as many times as you like and as often as you like. We are always growing, learning and developing as people. This is where I am currently when I played. Who I am a week from now may be the same but through different situations and encounters things will evolve. That's the beautiful part about being you and knowing who you are and it's ok if it changes. In all honesty, your I am section will change.

All throughout my life I was made to feel that being all over the place was a bad thing and that I didn't know what I wanted. I would share my dreams and would hear, "You just all over the place; you don't know what you want." In fact, I did know exactly what I wanted. I just discovered I wanted more than most. It always felt negative when I heard those words and most would probably agree. When someone says you are all over the place it is usually not a good thing.

But I decided to change things up a bit and turn a negative into a positive. I decided being all over the place doesn't have to be a bad or negative thing at least not to me anyway. I said that going forward when people told me I was all over the place it just meant I would be international someday. Now, don't get me wrong, I had to get help organizing my thoughts so I hired an assistant, sort of a project manager. My very own "Kim Possible" because she makes it possible.

My desire to try new things is unparalleled in comparison to most. My list of things to do, businesses to start and things to try is longer than long. I look at it this way, when I get up in age, I will be able to say I tried almost everything I desired and started all kinds of businesses. I am a true serial entrepreneur. I have sold all kinds of things. Started all kinds of businesses. People would often say what don't you sell and my answer is and always will be, there are only two things for sure I will never sell (comma pause for effect) and that's drugs and my behind. I just won't sell those two. As for anything else, it's up for debate.

But back to this ice breaker and who I am, well-being grammatically correct Who am I! You see I am me and I'm super silly, loving and kind as my bestie says. There I go being all over the place again! Ok let's focus. This is a leadership and personal development book. I am the person that heard my little sister say in conversation, "I just applied for this job, I hope I get it" then I said with a raised excited voice, "Girl you better claim that job!" "That's right sister motivate me!" she said in full excitement with me! After we got off the phone, I continued driving up I-95N headed back to SC from Florida for my 29th birthday vacation. I said my sister motivates me and the motivate me movement was born! I came up with all the awesome free motivation for the back. It was amazing but don't let me forget to mention that I listened to the book "The Secret" on CD the whole way down to the Florida Keys. So, I guess you can say that the "Motivate Me" movement was inspired by the book "The Secret" by Rhonda Byrne. I never thought about that until now. See we are always learning and evolving and seeing things through a new set of eyes. You can listen to the same book or motivational speech over and over again and get something different each time. It all depends on what chapter of your life you're currently in or what part of the storm. You see, you're either in a storm, coming out of a storm or about to go into a storm. There is so much more to me but you pretty much get that I'm pretty cool, very determined and ambitious!

I love hair. It's my passion and my first love. I don't care how many other businesses I start, hair is my foundation, the roots to my tree, the sugar to my sweet tea. Ok ok ok I know I'm doing the most but again that's what makes me, me. I tend to keep it real and like to have fun. However, I know who I am and how to read the room and act accordingly.

As an ice breaker for a small group be it a leadership training, new hire orientation, or even the first day of school, who am I is sure to be a hit. I would have my group or even a single participant say my client while I'm styling their hair to give themselves a round of applause after they finish like seriously clap for yourself. Think about it, when was the last time you gave yourself a round of applause? Then we would share what we wrote on each side; this is the real fun part. When doing this exercise people almost always draw a blank and they say aloud to themselves "Who am I?" My response when I see their delay in writing once the timer is set, is to say aloud, "Who are you? Only you can answer that question." I gently tell them how many minutes are left and when there is 30 seconds and the final 10 second countdown. You will be surprised what you write down as well as your peers. It's especially fun with kids of all ages. But wait, it's a two-part game. That's right, the second part of the game goes like this: you turn the paper over and write I am at the top of the paper and set another 3-minute timer and I then tell them to write down all their goals and dreams as if they were already a reality. Its manifestation time for the next 3 minutes. I really think this game should be mandatory for everyone every three months at a minimum, so you keep your goals fresh as well as keep your mental health in check.

What I do

Now that you know who I am let's talk a little about what I do. What do you say when someone asks you what you do? Do you have to think about it or do you have your elevator speech ready at all times? Can you spit it out in 30-60 seconds or do you fumble and give too much information? It's important at all stages of life to be able to explain what you do quickly. Remember presentation is 95% of what you do and if you stay ready you never have to get ready. It's better to be prepared for an opportunity and not have an opportunity than to have an opportunity and not be prepared.

I like to say I comb hair. It usually warrants a smile or look of confusion. Either way, an explanation is expected. One day while in the salon my suite mate and I came up with the acronym for comb because I say it so much plus, I'm just extra like that!

C - I Care for hair I'm also a character lol

O - I'm Optimistic

M - I'm a natural Motivator

B - I'm going to bring out the Beautiful Me in you! (My salon slogan)

I like to say that part of my mission and purpose in life is to motivate, encourage and inspire people to follow their dreams. I wrote a paper in my freshman year, my only year, at Benedict College entitled, "Why on Earth am I Here," for my freshman seminar class. It was the weirdest thing, not the paper. That's when I first discovered how I Journal. I knew the exact time stamp. I inserted the paper below because I put it in a plastic sleeve in a notebook because I knew I would reflect back and share it with the world one day. I always say one day isn't on the calendar but here we are, so that proves anything is possible.

Before you read the paper from my younger self, I want you to know that if you haven't discovered your purpose or mission, it's ok, it will come to you when you least expect it. I was 19 years old when I first discovered one of my purposes because I believe you can have more than one. The students would tell me that I motivated or inspired them on campus during conversations and I was honestly taken aback. All I did was share some of my goals and dreams. It wasn't that big of a deal at least not to me, but I have to take into consideration that I have always been told my goals were lofty, and before you google it like I did when I was told that it means big, high, soaring but that's me. I think I took it to heart when they said if you're going to dream, DREAM BIG!

It may be time for you to ask yourself and write down on paper why on earth am I here? it's grammatically incorrect but remember this was my 19-year-old self so be kind to her. We all have these different parts of ourselves, something I learned in therapy. I would suggest being loving and kind like my best friend always says to all the parts of yourself. Remember he/she (your past self) got you this far.

Why on Earth am I here?
Erica McGee

Feb.17, 2004

Wed. 1pm

I feel I was placed on this earth for several reasons. Some of these reasons have already been revealed to me at the age of 19 years old. I didn't realize how big of an impact I had on people until someone told me that I inspired them. I feel I'm here to help people and to make a difference in people's lives by sharing my determination to reach my goals. I learned that by talking about my goals and taking action to achieve them this in turn affects the people around me. They see me doing things and they see the positive coming out of it and it inspires them to do things. I also tend to be a motherly figure and this helps people. And I believe that if I already haven't, I can save someone's life. So, I initially feel like I am here to help people aspire in life as well as aspire to great heights in my own life. I am going to get my degree and my cosmetology license and go on to do great things with those achievements. Such as owning my own salon and hair magazine. Which will be helping the economy by creating jobs and a positive work environment.

Once you have written down why on earth you believe you are here in your handy dandy notebook or journal, be sure to revisit and reread what you write.

I was always told two things growing up that ensured for a great work ethic. My daddy would say I don't care if you're the janitor you better be the best janitor you can be and that whatever you do you have to love it so much that you would do it for free. What I do, since we are on that subject matter, is build and grow by giving it away. What do I mean? Well since combing hair has never really felt like work, I decided if I was going to grow fast, I would have to get some skin in the game and give it away. I would create flyers on my computer or at the library. I would put 4 flyers on a page, print and cut them. The library would give you 10 free pages a day, so I would have 40 free flyers to pass out a day! The flyer would ask a question something like Are you looking for a new stylist? Then I would tell them to look no more call me, Ms. Precious, for your hair care needs. Specializing in healthy hair of all types. Book your appointment today. The first one is on the house. Which meant free, but I would still add the word free just to be clear. I would also add Restrictions Apply and tips are appreciated. Let's be clear and realistic: the free service was something that would only take me an hour or less. I built an entire clientele like this after I closed my salon and screen print shop. I didn't mind doing it for free because I knew I not only had to tithe in my finances but in my time and talent. Plus, since I became a professional best friend maker not only was I able to gain new clients I gained new friends. I met my Libra sister/best friend after doing her best friend's hair for free and then she came in for a free hair service and we have been best friends almost 10 years all from a free hair service. Going to the hairdresser every day can be amazing especially when you enjoy and love what you do, the conversations, that behind the chair flare and those shampoo bowl chronicles are things that I just can't make up like the lunch break baby, but that's another book. My time spent in the salon is almost always a good time.

Digging further into my journal I found a poem that I wrote and I decided to share in hopes to express how passionate I am about what I do. I believe it was around 21 or 22 years old when I created this piece.

My Love Letter to You

I love you so much. It feels so good to know you, to touch you, feel you, embracing you is my joy. I love it when you call me.

To wake up to you. Without you I would be lost in a world of confusion. If anyone takes you away from me, I would lyrically lose my mind.

You calm me down and soothe my soul.

You let me know that I can and that I am.

Because of you I can hold my head high. You do so much for me and you're always on my mind. You are so kind.

Sometimes you're rough or even coarse but you're always *Hawaiian Silky*. Your *Textures and Tones are of many*. You are *Dark and Lovely*. You're so *Soft and Beautiful*. You're full of *Blue Magic*. Your *Pink Lotion Lusters* with *African Pride* helps me find my *New Expressions* because you are *Just for Me*.

You're the love of my life. My artistic thoughts intertwined with you to create things unseen. Your colors send me on high. You're thick, thin, curly, straight, long, and even short.

You're my passion, not just fashion. You're my expression, you allow me to breathe through you.

You complete me

I love you forever and always

This is my love letter to you

She's All Over The Place

Written for my love of Hair

I remember sitting in the salon writing this poem about how much I loved hair and incorporating all the hair products I used thinking wow I really love hair.

I also wrote a 10-year plan to become a millionaire despite all the loopholes and lack of real direction. It really just let me know that since I was very young, I have always been very ambitious. If I motivate, inspire and encourage just one person I'm happy. That will mean I made a difference in someone's life.

Sometimes you really have to ask yourself What do I do and go a step further and say why do I do it? What am I passionate about? What do I love so much that I would do it for free yes, I said free. I have done more free hair than I can count. I actually did some free hair today and was tipped $50. The actual service was $75, not bad for a free service. I was a blessing to a young lady for her birthday which brought me great joy and fulfillment at the same time. I know I said I was a serial entrepreneur, but I did not list everything that I have sold or all the businesses I have started. I was actually called the ultimate entrepreneur in the Panorama newspaper. It was my 3rd feature in the paper.

So, as you know I'm a licensed cosmetologist for over 16 years. I just completed the barber crossover program which is what brought me to Texas. I will list my many ventures below:

BME Screen Printing

Proud Folks (Gay Pride apparel and accessories)

The Produce Lady

Licensed life insurance agent

KP's Lemonade

Food vendor at festivals

Novelty vendor at festivals

Meal prep business

Photographer

Motivational speaker at events

Author

The beautiful me dream team and the BME ambassadors (2 Mentorship programs with local colleges in Columbia, SC)

Personal assistant to James "JT" Thomas, Steve Harvey's retired personal barber of 30 plus years

So now that you know a little bit about what I do and have done it's time for you to discover what's in it for you

What's in it for you?

That's an easy one! You're in for a treat and a whole lot of great leadership and personal development skills and lessons. I'm in the opportunity business. This book will give you the opportunity to learn what I learned from some of my great mentors as well as learn from some of my mistakes in business and in life.

You will learn that one of the first things you need to do is find a mentor or 3 or recognize who your mentors are in life. The people that are doing what you want to do successfully and who are willing to share their knowledge with you. They are usually willing to share said knowledge because it's fulfilling to them, you're paying them, or they will be compensated on the back end from what they are teaching and sharing with you in some way. Do know that something is in it for them as well. I have had all types of mentors and coaches in my career and I still have them. It's also ok to know that some of your mentors will come and go, some will be in your life for a lifetime and some for a season. Be ok with that and just soak up what you're supposed to learn like a sponge, a new fresh out of the pack sponge, not an old used up sponge that is holding on to bacteria aka negative thinking.

Always go in with a positive mental attitude. I learned that from a mentor that I will never meet because he has been dead for more than 50 years. Some of your mentors will be authors and speakers to whom you will never meet. So, let's recap the definition of mentor really quick. A mentor is an experienced guide or advisor aka someone who has already done what you are trying or attempting to do.

So, let's see what else is in it for you? I mean that's a lot right there but I also would love for you to become a part of the Motivate Me movement and you can do so by following us on all social media platforms and signing up for our awesome subscription box that I believe will change the way schools and non-profits do fundraisers, scholarships and the way we appreciate who and what motivates us and so much more. Remember it's a movement. A movement that started with someone looking me in my eyes and telling me

I was all over the place and that I didn't know what I wanted. Always remember you can turn a negative into a positive. There is also an amazing opportunity awaiting you at the end of this book.

My glass isn't half full or half empty. It's overflowing. I'm just waiting for my pour and when it comes to giving you always give from your overflow not from your cup. What's in your cup is for you what's in your saucer, the overflow, is what you give to others. I'm sure you have seen people give almost all of themselves to people's projects and even their businesses and there's nothing left for themselves. Trust me I know; I was that person.

Well, if you like what you have read or heard so far don't stop now it's about to be juicy.

Lesson: Know Who You Are

Knowing who you are is so important, especially at a young age. We are all impressionable, however, we must have a solid foundation for our values.

Chapter 2

THE COW AND THE RHINO AT THE WAFFLE HOUSE

Cows and rhinos at the waffle house? What's this chapter about? I know that's what you're probably thinking, but just hold on we will get to that in a moment.

The purpose of this chapter and what I would like you to take away is the importance of mentorship, friendship and being seen and heard aka speak up. Closed mouths don't get fed! Understand the importance of reading and developing yourself. But not just reading anything, I'm talking about reading books that will change your life.

Ask yourself this question: What is my thought process about personal development and leadership training?

This is an area of your life, in my opinion, that you should never stop developing.

Now let's get to these cows and rhinos! That's right let's jump straight into the juicy stuff!

It was my younger 19-year-old self that left the house and said that I couldn't come home until I had a job. Like seriously, someone had to hire me on the spot or I couldn't let myself come home. Sure, enough, I found a job that day. I was hired on the spot at a Waffle House on Broad River Rd. in Columbia, SC late Spring, early Summer after my second semester of college. I had only been working there a few weeks, maybe a month, when two gentlemen walked in with suites, ties and briefcases. They seated themselves, their server set them up and took their order. In the meantime, I observed them discussing what looked like serious business. I was always told that I talked too much but I also knew that closed mouths don't get fed and I'm always hungry. I took my 19-year-old self over and asked them what they were talking about, even though my coworker whose table they were seated at told me to leave them people alone.

The question he asked before telling me changed my life forever. He said, "Are you a Cow or a Rhino?" I thought about it for about 3 seconds and I said I'm a Rhino now what does that mean and what are y'all talking about? Mr. Bernard Gaddist would become one of my best mentors. I say one of my mentors because each of the mentors I have taught me the best of what they knew which helped groom me. I have many mentors, but Mr. Gaddist laid a solid foundation for me that was full of leadership and development skills that would serve me for a lifetime. He gave me so many books to read about leadership, building a business, personal and self-development, team building and so much more. I remember sitting in the salon after completing hair school reading, "How to Win Friends and Influence People" by Dale Carnegie. This is one of my favorite books and people would ridicule me and mock me for reading a book with such a title. They would say why would you want to win friends and influence people? I was 21 years old by this time and I didn't know how to answer. I just put my head down and kept reading. I didn't know at the time it would lead me to become a professional best friend maker! However, I did know that I was learning valuable skills, one of which I will never forget. The writer said if there are 2 people and one has 2 friends and the other has 10 friends and they both need to borrow $100, which friend is more likely to get the $100? One can only ask 2 friends for $50 each or each friend for $100 whereas the other can ask each friend for $10 each or 5 friends for $20 or 4 friends for $25. I learned that you can get people to do almost anything by allowing them to think they are doing it for themselves. We think about ourselves 95% of the time even if we are doing things for others because we are doing it for our own satisfaction. Learning the power of winning friends and influencing people was definitely life changing.

He also gave me a cassette tape that I still possess by Jerry Clark, "Murphy's Committee." I'm surprised it still plays after all these years and how many times I have played it, flipping it over and over in hopes to gain some insight on whatever chapter of my life I was in at the time. Mr. Gaddist also introduced me to the world of multilevel marketing. He took me to a conference where I met my first millionaire, Chris Gardner. Yep, he is the Pursuit of Happyness guy. If it wasn't for me rereading a journal entry a few months ago, I wouldn't have even remembered that he was the first millionaire that I had met. So journaling is super important and more importantly rereading those journals. Mr. Gaddist exposed me to another world of possibilities. I am forever thankful for the cows and rhinos at the waffle house and that I asked the right question to the right person. To this day I ask my mentees and my clients if they are cows or rhinos.

I discovered that you could listen and watch motivational videos on YouTube. Les Brown is and always will be one of my all-time favorites. I discovered Les and countless other speakers on platforms like YouTube. Les explained in a video that a Chinese bamboo tree takes five years to break through the ground, once it breaks ground it can grow 90 feet tall in just 5 weeks. I was down and out for about five years but it felt like an eternity because very few knew of my struggles. I had experienced what I had then called failure in the second year of my printing company and was trying to recover from what I learned is called accelerated business growth. We will touch more on that in later chapters. After 5 long years of trying to get back right, as I like to say, I

> Erica, I watched your bamboo tree grow underneath the earth for years. Now you broke the surface. Your growth potential is unlimited.
>
> -Bernard Gaddist

was blessed with an opportunity and relocated and have since broken ground. I reached out to Mr. Gaddist and informed him that not only was I all over the place, but I would also soon be a published author. His response reflected what I heard Les Brown say on countless occasions in his teachings.

Let me share with you how I ended up at a waffle house with said rhinos and cows in the first place.

After the first semester at Benedict College, I was super proud of myself especially since I passed a math class in college that I failed in high school. However, I really didn't know and understand how the whole money thing worked in college. I received my acceptance letter for college the week

I graduated from high school. I was already enrolled to attend Fayetteville Beauty College and working in a salon my senior year all while completing my internship at the board of education for the academy of finance program, which I was in my entire four years of high school. I have always been an overachiever. I even remember going into the interview with my friend saying I'm going to get this job. They are going to hire me! But I digress. It's now the second semester and the financial aid office had requested I go to the white house. Not that white house, the white house is where you went to either give them some money or get some money. In my case, I was told my financial aid had run out. Of course, I had a pure look of confusion on my face because when my mother dropped me off, we did the paperwork and I thought everything was good. This is why it's so important to get educated about how money works at a young age and how college works.

I was told I had two options which were get a gap loan or go home. This college thing was just starting to get good. I definitely wasn't going back to Fayetteville, NC. No ma'am, no ham, no turkey, that was not about to happen, so I signed that paper so fast. So, we solved that problem but as you know there is always another one waiting to arise.

To know me is to know I love hair. My college best friend always says I describe people by their hair first, which is true. Jessica and I both lived on the 6th floor at Mather Hall and we clicked instantly. Jessica would always say you could smell the pump it up when you got off the elevator. LOL! People would often ask me if I even went to class because it seemed like all I did was hair, but I passed all my classes. However, I didn't believe in being a "broke college kid." We moved in on a Tuesday. I braided my roommate Keesha's hair Wednesday after we walked to Star Beauty World to purchase hair and supplies. I was booked by Thursday. My price was $10.00, but you got half off your first service! So that meant I was doing cornrows for $5,00, yes, I said $5.00 cornrows with hair added straight to the back. As I type this, I had a thought: man, I'm old; but I am only 36 years old. I was committed to not being a broke college kid!

The second semester was almost over and I already knew I wasn't going back to North Carolina. I had several jobs while attending college and I did hair in my dorm room. While at one of my many jobs, I inquired with one of my coworkers about cosmetology schools in the area and my coworker was actually enrolled at Kenneth Shuler School of Cosmetology, so I set up an appointment to talk to admissions. This was a critical time in my life because, after speaking to admissions, I had to make a decision. You see, there wasn't enough money for me to attend Benedict college to obtain my degree in business and marketing AND to obtain my cosmetology license. So, I decided and it was all up to me. I mean I could have called my mom or my dad or even my friends, but I had a decision to make. It was my life after all. So, I went with my heart and I called my mother and told her that I wasn't coming home. I was going to hair school.

While I waited for my start date at Kenneth Shuler School of Cosmetology, I knew I had to find a job. I knew when I left the house that day to find said job, I would accomplish my goal and nothing could stop a will to win. I said I would find a job that day and that's exactly what I did. What I didn't know is that I would be sharing how cows and rhinos at the Waffle House would change my life and maybe even yours.

Ask yourself, are you a cow or a rhino and what does that even mean? Do I have mentors to advise me in the different areas of my life? What is the importance of mentorship?

Lesson: The Power of Mentorship

Mentorship is powerful on so many levels. Not only does it help prepare you for life and help you avoid some of life's pitfalls, but the right mentorship really can plant seeds of wisdom, courage, self-sufficiency, discernment, humility, growth and development on insurmountable levels.

I'm more than proud of you for discovering the power of mentorship and I'm excited for what new doors this newfound information is going to open for your life and career.

Chapter 3

THE GREEN JOLLY RANCHER

I vowed to never eat another green jolly rancher again in my life! So, seeing that I'm all over the place let's take this chapter down memory lane to my childhood...

My mother sent my brother to the store, so being his kid sister, I tagged along.

We were born in Springfield, IL, but had since moved down south to the Carolinas. Our neighbor Quincy joined us and we lived in a duplex on Bunce Rd. in Fayetteville, NC. Before we left, I asked my mom for some money. "Girl I ain't got no money," words we have almost all heard when we asked our parents for money. We walked to the store and once we arrived, I found myself digging in those red bins on the lower shelves where the penny candy was located. I looked to my left and I looked to my right, no one was in sight, so I quickly popped the green jolly rancher in my mouth. Back down the street we walked. "Precious!" Quincy yelled my name. "What's that?" I was minding my business enjoying my good green "free" jolly rancher. It was only .10 cents. I figured the owner wouldn't miss a dime. "What's in your mouth? Oooooohhhhh, imma tell your momma!"

I quickly spit the jolly rancher out into the long green grass that was on the side of the road that we walked on to get back home. After we got home Quincy did exactly what he said he was going to do; he told my mama. Linda, my beloved mother, proceeded to get up and walk her child "me" back down the street to pay for said green jolly rancher but not before making me look for that very green jolly rancher in the tall green grass on the side of the road where I disposed of my sweet treat. However, the evidence was on my tongue, so I couldn't deny the accusation, plus lying was never something I was very good at, so I just tell the truth. After we walked to the store to pay for the jolly rancher, my mother made me apologize to the man for taking his merchandise even though it was only $.10 cent it was his $.10 cent. I vowed to never steal again. We headed back home but not before my mom made me look for that green Jolly rancher one more good time in that tall green grass on the side of the road. By this time, it was dark and needless to say, I didn't find the jolly rancher, nor did I ever steal or eat a green jolly rancher again. Thanks Ma!

I decided that I would become an entrepreneur after I learned how to spell the word in the 3rd grade. I spent time with my father as a child going to yard sales, buying things and taking old things to the flea market to sell them. Browsing wholesale catalogs looking for merchandise to resale. Saturday mornings were the best so long as you woke up on time because my daddy would definitely leave you at the house. But that was not a problem for me. I always met him at the car for our Saturday morning yard sale and flea market activities.

If I wanted money from my parents, especially my dad, I had to work for it, and by work, I mean cut the grass, wash his car, iron his clothes, or make him a hot plate of food. But I didn't mind because it felt good to work for what I wanted. I knew it was mine because I earned it myself. After I became an entrepreneur at the age of 21 years old by becoming a licensed cosmetologist, I decided I was going to earn a six-figure income. It's easy, I said to myself. I started calculating forwards and backwards. All I had to do was earn $8333.33 a month. Which was $2000 a week if you work 50 weeks a year, a man once told me only a slave works 52 weeks a year, so I subtracted two weeks for vacation. I figured if you work five days a week that's $400 a day and $50 an hour if you work eight hours a day. My average client at that time was around $50 each and I could take up to two clients an hour depending on the service. So that sounded pretty realistic for me as a licensed cosmetologist.

Moral of the story is you eat the elephant one bite at a time. Every inch is a cinch. Sometimes you have to hurry up and wait, don't be in a rush to get to a stoplight. Write down your goals, try using the SMART System. It stands for Specific, Measurable, Attainable, Realistic, and Time frame. I learned that from a project management course I took some years ago. Sometimes you really have to sit and reflect on your life. Really take a look over your life you will probably say wow I really am blessed.

God really is Good like real, real, real GOOD!

Last year this time I was homeless, (my name wasn't on a lease) living in a laundry room at an Airbnb in Irving, TX imagining this day TODAY! I would close my eyes and imagine laying in my bed in my beautiful town home or luxury apartment somewhere in Arlington TX as I had decided that's where I wanted to work and live. It would have all the amenities I wanted such as a garden tub, island in my kitchen, above cabinet space in my kitchen for decor, washer and dryer, jack and jill bathroom. I would decorate with pretty decor from stores like #homegoods #marshalls #ross #roomstogo #biglots #tjmaxx #ikea just to name a few. My pretty teapot would always sit on my stove, which happens to be light blue. I even got a fireplace which was a bonus! I also imagined doing a fancy #photoshoot for my one-year anniversary of living in the DFW, which I did. I printed a 18x24 of my favorite image from the shoot and placed it over my fireplace.

As I reflect on the past two years of my life here in the #dfw all I can say is wow #God is good. He will restore what you lost 1000-fold as my Pastor says! I am forever thankful and #humbled by all the opportunities for growth and development, especially the lesson I learned from the green jolly rancher

> **Lesson:** Expect the Unexpected
> I didn't expect that as a little girl I would steal a green jolly rancher and learn a life lesson from it, however I am thankful for my attitude of gratitude towards all of life's many situations and lessons.

Chapter 4
5AM FLASHLIGHT

The titles of these chapters are all over the place just like me so let's talk about the flashlight at 5am and how that impacted my life.

I was enrolled in beauty college but decided to take three months off from hair school to save money to get my 1st apartment. I had several jobs, one of which required me to be up before dawn so I walked to work at 5am with a flashlight because there were no street lights and it was dark. I worked at a chicken and biscuit place called Bojangles. After work, I would then walk back home past the hair school that I was attending to go home and change, then go to another job and work all night.

Always ask yourself what have you learned from this and each situation you have been faced with? If you go in with this mindset you will always win. I don't want you to just hear me, but I want you to listen. You have overcome more obstacles than you realize, but you still believe you are your worst critic. Today, I would like to free you of that myth so you can become your best critic. Take note that no matter how big or small the accomplishment, you are doing the dang thing! Look in the mirror and say hey beautiful or hey handsome I'm proud of you, you're doing a great job, you got this!

My roommate at the time informed me we wouldn't be renewing the lease so that meant I needed to be looking for an apartment asap. I was 19 or 20 years old in a new city and had no clue how to go about getting an apartment, but I knew I would figure it out. I sat down with Ms. Marilyn, she was the school accountant, and I asked her what my options were because I knew I would need to take some time off and work two maybe even three jobs to save enough money to get my own place and to get another car as my engine blew in my car months earlier. I'm in this new city with no car, no family, nothing but my faith, ambition, and will to win. She told me I could take three months off and come back so I said that's what I will do. I applied for several jobs all located within a 15 to 30-minute walk from where I was staying. I got hired at Bojangles. Then, I was hired at a call center that was located behind the apartment so it was perfect. I devised a plan. I grabbed my handy dandy notebook and I began to write. I will work these two jobs and save a few thousand dollars for my car, 1st month's rent and deposit, then I will finish cosmetology school. Surprisingly enough that's exactly what I did. Why do I say surprisingly you may ask? Because I had planned all kinds of things and they didn't work out. That's all a part of life. Sometimes plans don't go as we would like or expect them to but on occasion things will work out. Appreciate those times and cherish them by paying attention to what you learned about yourself.

I learned so much about myself at that young age. How often do you sit and reflect on the younger parts of yourself? How ambitious, fearless, and bold you were. That part of you is still inside you, YOU just have to reach inside and ignite him/her.

I reported to work so early that I would have to leave the house at 5 am to make it on time to open the store. I tried cabs, and of course, Uber and Lyft were nonexistent back in the day, at least not in South Carolina. The cabs wouldn't come get me because it was too close and it wasn't worth the trip. So, I grabbed a flashlight because the streetlights didn't work and I walked up the hill and down the street to my job because the way I saw it, what other choice did I have? I called my mom at the end of my first year in college and told her I wasn't coming home. I was going to cosmetology school and she said OK, you are grown. So, my grown self did what I had to do to accomplish my goals.

I would arrive at work bright eyed and bushy tailed just as bright and chipper as I wanted to be. They would almost always have me work the drive thru. My regulars loved me. I worked that drive thru you hear me! "Thank you for choosing Bojangles. Would you like to try a Cajun filet biscuit combo?" There wasn't a day that went by that a customer wouldn't say how are you so chipper this early in the morning? I would just smile and think to myself I woke up this morning and someone didn't. My daddy always told me it doesn't matter what job you're doing, if you're going to do it, you better do it right and to the best of your abilities.

After a long day of slinging chicken, I would walk home around lunch time, which meant I no longer needed my flashlight. My school would be open and I would almost always see my classmates outside, so I would smile and wave and say to myself you will be back soon just keep working and saving it's going to happen. Then I would go home, change and go to the call center from 4 - 11pm and be back up at 4am to do it all over again. The call center was so big and with little to no thought, I immediately started telling everyone I was in hair school and that I was available to take care of their hair care needs.

Those three months went by pretty fast and sure enough, I went back to school after moving into my new apartment and getting my car. It was an amazing feeling. One of my classmates looked at me and said, "I guess you got a story to tell now huh?" It wasn't until years later that I actually listened to her words when I was telling the story in the salon to a client that I had an epiphany, like a real ah ha moment. Yes, I did have a story to tell and so do you. When it's time to tell it you will know because it will be a good story to tell especially if you're young.

I graduated hair school on my 21st birthday in the fall and I was ready to see what all life had to offer. I found the salon I wanted to work in before I even enrolled in hair school. I braided the hair of the owner, Sonia, (Ms. "DJ" Richardson), in my dorm room in the spring the year prior. She had the prettiest hair line of any client I had ever styled. She was pregnant with her youngest son. I remember telling her I'm going to hair school when this semester ends and I'm going to come work at your salon. She smiled and said OK. My bestie and I would take the bus to her shop or I would drive, depending on whether my car was cooperating that day. I think I stalked DJ for about a year and a half about working with her. She would tell me if she had to build me a station I would have somewhere to work. I started working with her shortly after graduating hair school. Sonia, (Ms. "DJ" Richardson), took me under her wing and taught me everything she knew. We maintain a relationship to this day. She is my hair mommy and healthy hair care mentor.

Whatever your career path is, my suggestion is to find a mentor in that field and latch on so you can learn all you can.

Put in some sweat equity. Find out what areas they need help in and see where you can be of service by volunteering your time and efforts. The more good you put out, the more good you will receive. It's true: you reap what you sow. The struggle was real and I was faced with a challenge and I overcame it. Think back to when you faced an obstacle and overcame it. I will wait a moment...

Now put this book down and give yourself a round of applause. Stop so you can really put the book down and clap for yourself (listens to the sound of my awesome readers clapping for themselves). We are so hard on ourselves and onto the next thing that we don't acknowledge how great, gifted and talented we are. You are your best critic because going forward you will take note of how dope you are, how consistent and determined you are because you are winning even when it doesn't seem like you are winning. I believe in you and I know YOU believe in you.

> **Lesson**: I guess you have a story to tell huh? Don't just Hear, Listen...
>
> We all have a story to tell and I promise you will know when it's time to tell that story! We are halfway through guys. Go grab a snack, something to drink and keep reading or listening! You got this!

Chapter 5
GET OFF THE PANIC BUTTON

Ask yourself this question: what decisions am I resisting or panicking about in life and business?

I went to church that morning with a heavy heart. I had a big decision to make. After hearing the title of the sermon and the message, I was sure I wasn't supposed to move. I consulted with my friend Jerome who was my photographer at the time and told him I wasn't going to move and rent the building. He heard the same message that Sunday as we were also church members. I had been deliberating on whether I should open my own salon and portrait studio. Jerome's words after I told him that Pastor said get off the panic button, so I wasn't going to move changed my life. He said the Pastor said get off the panic button, but he didn't say be still! In obedience I signed my lease for 2 years. I signed a longer lease to get a reduction in the rent. I moved in along with Jerome and Beautiful Me Hair Salon and Portrait studio was born that August. It grew rather fast. My clientele picked up and because I'm all over the place, I knew it was time to bring my other dreams to life: mentorship programs, hair magazine and my printing company. I remember the day my best friend Jessica, that's the college best friend, called me and said, "You're still going to start your magazine, right?" It was kind of like she was asking and telling me at the same time because that's what best friends do! Sure enough, I started working on my magazine but with no real plan or guidance. I just jumped right in headfirst because, remember, I know how to swim and what is the worst that can happen. Well, let's see, a lot of wasted time, resources and money that's what. If you would have just done your research, you could have saved time and money as well as the time it takes to heal and recoup said money.

> Do your research before you jump into a new project. The water may look deep but can be very shallow and misleading.

Things had really picked up in the salon so much that I decided it was time to go to the next level and hire not only a shampoo assistant but a salon manager. Things were flowing very well and I was on track to bring in six figures which was my goal. I had already done the calculations. Let me break it down for you again. If you work 50 weeks a year and earn $2,000 a week, that's $100K a year. Some of you, especially my stylist and barbers, are probably already doing this and don't realize it because you don't see it and this could be because we are not properly keeping our books. But that's another chapter or maybe even another book! The Struggle is Real...Real Life Topics: I earn six figures and I'm broke!

After getting off the panic button, as instructed, opening the salon and hiring a staff, I still wanted more. I wanted to grow and help more people all the while thinking about how I would eventually retire from behind the chair. I knew I wouldn't make my millions combing hair, but I loved what I did, how it made me feel and how I made my clients feel. After all, my clients had become my family. By this time the salon had what I called its very own dream team because I had read that without a team you cannot build your dream. That is what birthed the mentorship programs. Mr. Gaddist said in life there are things you can't afford not to be able to afford. So, creating the dream team wasn't optional for me. I mean it really wasn't. I was up for over 24 hours writing the 17-page plan and overview for what the mentorship program would consist of. My 7th grade teacher, Ms. Leeks, said I had been impregnated with that thing!

People would always ask me what made me get into the printing industry? I almost always say, "Because I always say I'm going to put that on a shirt!" Because your business is my business and you can't run your business successfully without marketing, which is one of my other passions. Every successful business owner will tell you, you must have a solid marketing plan or strategy in order to sustain your cashflow.

I had been playing around with different types of printing for years. Once I decided to go brick and mortar, it was time to take things up a notch. Of course, I did my research, but I had no real plan. Remember I know how to swim, so I jumped in head first again! In all actuality I had no idea what the hell I was doing. But I knew I could do anything I put my mind to and I knew I had a work ethic like no other. Like the greats say, "You will not outwork me, you may be smarter and even have more money than me, but you will not and I mean will not outwork me!" So, I went to work, I ordered equipment and watched YouTube videos connected with other printers. I was determined to figure this print thing out. You see I love hair; I mean I loooooooove me some hair, but I also wanted to make sure I explored other options and things that I was interested in doing. This is when people begin to tell you

you're all over the place. Having multiple ideas, goals and dreams doesn't necessarily mean you're confused or off track and can't focus. That is the google definition of being all over the place, however, it does mean that you may be ready for a coach or project manager or maybe just a personal assistant. I remember going into Belk, shoe shopping, speaking to the associate and telling him I needed a personal assistant. I must have rambled on so that he said you need an assistant for your thoughts. We both laughed and I agreed with him because my mind goes a mile a minute. I truly believe in my free motivation, especially the part that says you are brilliant and a genius. I feel like I come up with ideas that could really change the world. I'm sure you probably feel the same way sometimes.

However, this is still where people decide that you're all over the place. You just don't know what you want to do, you need to focus on one thing! Like most of us creatives, we ain't, yes, I said ain't, trying to hear that. We want it all and we want to do it all and that's final. You're probably shaking your head in agreement. I learned that you could have multiple projects going on at a time however you have to set a time to work on each project. If you don't know how to be a project manager then you go take a project management course or you hire one! If you think you can't afford to hire one, then find one you can barter with because if you want these dreams to become a reality then you can't afford not to be able to afford what you need to grow and expand your business.

> Focus on what you're good at and hire people in your areas of weakness.

When the student is ready the teacher will appear

So, I was doing this printing thing and loving it all while still doing hair. My creative juices were running full force. I printed 5,000 bright lime green and purple flyers and I started putting them all over town. Keep in mind, I have no real business plan, no real idea of what I'm doing, but I'm marketing my butt off because that's my strength. I received a call from a gentleman asking if I do bulk printing. I had no real idea what bulk printing was, so I asked the amount he was interested in having printed and I honestly don't remember the number. I just remember the conversation after that which took place at his print shop. Jabari, owner of Perfect Printing, picked up one of my flyers and called me to size up the competition, it's called market research. Once he realized there was no real competition seeing as I was such a newbie and had been calling around to other print shops hopelessly looking for someone to take me under their wing and show me the ropes, he did just that and became my big brother in the print industry.

I am forever thankful for my big bro in the print industry. Whenever you are getting ready to take on a new adventure, I suggest you keep in mind that you will make greater strides with a mentor (I have said this a whole bunch of times and I will say it more times because I truly want it to sink in). Sometimes it will just happen and other times you will have to seek one out. However, if a connection is made, it should flow and be mutually beneficial to both parties. A win-win situation if you will. Over the years not only did I learn from him and other printers, but I outsourced a great deal of my work to him which is what he suggested I do from the beginning, but I had already jumped in the water headfirst. So, he then suggested different equipment for me to purchase so that my work would be more efficient and not wash off. Yes, when I first started, I would get all sorts of calls about the print washing off because the images were not cured properly. I didn't have the proper oven to dry the images on the shirts, towels and bags.

Business was booming, the beautiful me dream team marketed for the salon and the BME ambassadors marketed for the screen print shop. We had it going on. I had unpaid and paid interns from Benedict College, Allen University and one from Midlands Technical College, which made up my two mentorship programs and I was happy as could be. I can honestly say that the first two years were a breeze outside of all the mistakes I made but that's to be expected in the first two years, right? I will never forget the time I printed 100 white shirts with purple ink. Then I looked back at the invoice and it was 100 purple shirts with white ink. Easy mistake, right? Yep and I had to eat that mistake. It only cost me a few hundred bucks and a few man hours. But as a good businesswoman I had to fulfill the order as requested. Even though I did try to sell the shirts, they didn't want them because that's not what they ordered.

> The student was ready and the teacher appeared.

I encountered all sorts of things, especially in the printing business. I didn't win a shirt bid for one cent, yes, I lost a short order by one shiny penny on the dollar. But that's business; it's not personal. I can honestly say I learned the true essence of being a real business owner when I opened BME Screen Printing. It was a completely different world from the beauty industry. I knew I didn't want to be self-employed forever. Real business owners can walk away from their business for an entire year and come back and it will still be running at least that was what I believed after learning about the four ways to legally earn money. At the tender age of 26, I learned that I didn't fully understand how long it takes to build that kind of sustainability. Even though I taught my mentees the difference between delayed and instant gratification, I was about to microwave my business and experience accelerated business growth and didn't even know it. I was driven by the fear of failing in my first two years of operating the printing business.

> **Lesson**: Obedience is better than sacrifice and sometimes you have to do it afraid. You will thank yourself later, but you must take the first step. Let's not forget to be loving and kind to yourself when you are the player that fumbles the ball and loses the game in the last play. Failure is the opportunity to begin again more intelligently.

Chapter 6
THE LADY ON THE BILLBOARD

I know you from somewhere. I would begin to think back in my mind and try to place their face, but it wasn't happening because half the people that stopped me and said these words were recognizing me from the billboards. I had them all over town for my printing company BME Screen Printing. I was the lady on the billboard. I could be in the grocery store and people would say you're the lady on the billboard. Or hey Ms. Motivation from the many motivational videos I shared on social media. The boards were only up for about a year, but I heard those words for years.

I remember saying I'm going to have a billboard and a full staff and three phone lines! I was so excited because business was booming. I called the company that sold the billboards and they sent out an agent. I told him I would be the easiest sale he would ever get because I knew exactly what I wanted, where I wanted it and my graphics team would handle all my artwork. Pretty simple, cut and dry, at least I thought, until he pulled up to my office and asked me to ride down Two Notch with him; so, I agreed.

He began to explain that he sold me the wrong board, well the wrong side of the board. He apologized several times, but I wasn't budging; I wanted what I wanted and I said if you can't give me the board I want then I don't want a billboard at all. The particular board I had chosen had visibility from 3 directions and the board he sold me only had visibility from one direction so that was a no go, at least until he counter offered by giving me two small boards along with the original. I then countered again with only if you give me the board I originally wanted when the other person's contract is up and the company agreed. They even extended the time the boards were up so everything I manifested came to fruition. I literally had three phone lines and more business than I could handle.

Which leads me to discuss failure and the fear of failure. Some people experience fight or flight or even both. My fight was that I feared failing. I wanted to win so bad that I would do whatever it took because my work ethic was relentless! However, I learned that no matter who you are and how hard you work, you will get tired. That's when the flight will kick in, but remember, it's ok. It's ok; just repeat those words to yourself when you are struggling. It's ok may be your saving grace.

You're going to fail! Yes, I'm talking to you reading/listening to this right now. You are a failure at some things. No one is good at everything. I know you're like wow, I thought she said her nickname was Ms. Motivation and she just called me a failure. Don't be afraid to fail. Failure isn't an option because you have to fail your way to success. The real question is how good of a failure are you? How many times do you fail at something and keep going? Do you even begin because you're scared you're going to fail or are you like me and you feared failure so much that you increased your marketing and said you would have more business than you could handle? All the while not realizing that too much business can be as bad as not having any business if you're not structurally sound enough to be able to handle a large capacity of business coming in at one time.

I read somewhere that most small businesses fail in the first two years, so I got scared because I had just celebrated 2 years in business. I read later that they really failed in the first 3-5 years. However, I read what I read and the fear of failing caused me to make my dreams a reality or somewhat of a nightmare.

Let me explain...

I didn't know the term for it at the time, but I suffered from accelerated business growth. I used to describe it as bottlenecking. Marketing was my thing. It was what I was supposed to get my degree in, but I left college after the first year to pursue my dream of becoming a licensed cosmetologist. Plus, there wasn't enough money (financial aid) for me to attend a 4-year college or university and cosmetology school. I really tried to do both and it wasn't happening. So, I went with my heart. Marketing came easy to me and it was actually fun for me.

If I had obtained my business and marketing degree, I might have heard, learned and understood the term accelerated business growth and what it can do to you and your business. Prior to this phase of my life that I categorized as "my biggest failure," it was also one of my greatest accomplishments. Not only did I accomplish my goal of owning and operating a printing company, I printed shirts, towels and bags for customers around the world and for schools and local businesses. I spoke at schools for pep rallies and career day. All before the age of 30 years old.

Again, we move so fast that we don't take time to acknowledge how amazing we are. I mean don't take your foot off the gas when you're on go, but don't drive so fast you get pulled over and get a ticket or that you crash and get into a wreck. I had my two mentorship programs that my friends and family helped me with that were operating successfully. We participated in local events and parades, fed the homeless and more. We even brought in speakers for the students at our monthly meetings.

After attending meetings at my local chamber of commerce and networking events at the Capital City Club, I won bids to print for my local airport. I learned about the different certifications and inclusions for women, LGBTQ and minority owned businesses. I learned that people do business with people they like and building relationships is super important. I learned that my love language is giving gifts. I love making people feel special plus I always leave a lasting impression. Remember, presentation is 95% of what you do and you only get one first impression. I almost never went to a meeting without a plant, some small gift or a bag of my business cards that had lollipops attached to them. I always leave a lasting impression and I'm pretty unforgettable like that. However, I had a decision to make because things had taken a turn for the worst. I decided to break my lease and cut my losses. If you would have asked me at that time, I would have told you I felt like a complete failure; like I was the player that fumbled the ball and lost the Super Bowl and was on suicide watch. Yes, it was that serious.

I shut the doors to my business because I had too much business and was so overwhelmed that I began to decline. I was bottlenecking because there was so much business coming in. My team and I consistently posted and followed up with clients, but the disconnect came during the ordering and fulfillment process. I had no real way to structurally handle it all myself and my staff had to manually enter every order because there was no online ordering system. I couldn't take it anymore. I felt like a failure and a disappointment, by this time, the guilt and shame were settling in big time. I sought out business coaches and advisors, but my emotions were all over the place. Every day I walked across the threshold of the building, I would cry, then I would leave, because I didn't want customers to come in and see me cry. My fight or flight was in overdrive. I didn't understand what was happening. I had a very successful salon, printing company and I can honestly say I didn't see this coming. I experienced so much guilt, shame and I felt so defeated that it wasn't until now that I am ready to share this with the world. I had several other entrepreneurs make comments and statements, some of which hurt because I already felt bad enough and felt like a failure. I decided after my rent check didn't clear the bank that I would move out of the building. So, I moved everything into a storage unit and sold some of my salon and printing equipment to seek higher ground because I was drowning in $30k worth of debt. I didn't ask for an extension on my rent; I just told him I was leaving and he said he understood.

As a young entrepreneur I created my own perception of what failure and success meant to me. I was so scared to fail from not having enough business that I increased my marketing and failed from having too much business. As stated, earning six figures was simply a must and it was the prerequisite to my dreams. When you're not the smartest in the room, you have to be the hardest working person in the room and my work ethic, as the young people would say, was sick. I worked earlier and later than anyone else I knew.

Some people say do it afraid and I partially agree because you will be afraid sometimes. Now wait a minute, this is a learning and leadership moment. I say I partially agree because if you write it down and make it plain then you shouldn't be afraid. In other words, you recruit a team and build a solid foundation. No excuses about what you can't afford. I'm here to tell you that you can't afford not to be able to afford what you need in life. There is always a way. So, if you have done your due diligence, what is there to be afraid of, says the fearless leader. However, there are all kinds of things to be afraid of such as soon as you sign your lease within the first 30 days someone breaks into your business, steals your laptop and trashes the building. I will never forget that day. I sat in the building on the floor and cried like a baby. Once I fixed my face, as my mother would say, I cleaned up, went to the store and purchased a new laptop. Clients, friends and family asked if I had insurance and of course I did because it was a lease requirement. The deductible was $1000, but the missing property didn't total that amount plus I didn't have $1000 liquid for a deductible. I can't say this enough: If you save money, one day money will save you. You're either in a crisis, coming out of a crisis or about to go into one. The key is to be as prepared as you can at all times.

I had made up my mind that I was going to be successful not realizing that I already was successful. I couldn't see the forest for the trees. I was 28 years old with a full staff of employees, interns and service-learning students from local schools and colleges. I was running a salon, printing company, two mentorship programs and maintaining partnerships with the Richland County youth arbitration program as a volunteer for at risk teenage girls. My company grossed $136k a year and I did this all before the age of 30 years old. But I wasn't satisfied because to some, that sounded like a lot or even like I may be bragging. To me at that time, it just wasn't enough because I wasn't earning money in my sleep. My business was not self-sustaining. My goal was to franchise BME Screen Printing and make it a household name with M3: The Motivate Me movement. I had a plan! At least I thought I did. They always say if you want to make God laugh, tell Him your plans.

I shut the doors to my business because I now understand, that chapter of my life had come to an end and it was time to move on despite how I looked to others. At the end of the day, I knew I had to do what was best for me at the time.

I was so attached emotionally to my business that I had a hard time processing and letting go as well as forgiving myself for making the mistakes I was meant to make. They were all lessons. My 7th grade teacher Ms. Leeks always told me she would see my face on the cover of a magazine but I decided to put it on a billboard; being fast as my momma would say!

> **Lesson**: Learning and Understanding the power of accelerated business growth. This time in my life was honestly one of the most challenging. I learned how to hurry up and wait. Exercise delayed gratification; it will be worth it in the end. You can't bake a cake in the microwave. At least, not a good one.

> *For I know the thoughts that I think toward you, saith the Lord, thoughts of peace, and not of evil, to give you an expected end.*
>
> Jeremiah 29:11

Chapter 7
THE DAY BEFORE 31

October 4th. It was around 6:30am EST on a Sunday I believe. I looked at my phone and I had several missed calls, a few from my sister Sparkle that lived in Texas and several from a random number. Of, course I called my sister back first to see why she called me at such an odd time because it was definitely out of the ordinary. You ok, she said of course why wouldn't I be I questioned. I saw on the news that it was flooding really bad in South Carolina. "Girl we good," I responded against my better judgement. I didn't have a TV at the time as all I did was work and I was currently on a break from social media so I really didn't know what was going on in the world. I hadn't been out of the apartment that morning. Once I assured her that I was fine I returned the next missed call. The phone rang and a lady answered. "May I ask who this is?' I had a missed call from this number?"

"Precious, you need to get out of the apartment."

"Who is this?"

"This is your neighbor; the apartments have flooded."

"Are you serious?"

"Yes, look over the banister…. "

I did as instructed and sure enough, when I leaned over the banister of my town home, the contents of the first floor were floating around in my living room. I immediately packed a bag of clothes and grabbed the several hundred dollars in cash I always kept handy in case of emergencies. This was definitely an emergency. I gave my neighbor some cash for her and her daughter before I jumped in my truck. If I would have slept any longer or had not returned the missed calls, I would have lost more than my apartment. I would have lost my truck as well.

I'm not sure if it was a few months or maybe even a year prior, but a lady came to my salon and asked me if she could leave some pamphlets on homelessness and of course I said yes because my mentees would feed the homeless at least once a month. Giving back is super important to me. After reading the information I was taken aback not knowing that I too at the time, was homeless because my name wasn't on a lease. Being homeless doesn't always mean you are sleeping on the street or even in your car. I was staying with a friend, essentially renting his spare room, as we weren't really roommates because my name wasn't on the lease just months prior to the incident. I felt a little defeated and overwhelmed all over again. Here goes another traumatic, life changing event in less than a year. To top it off, I'm about to be homeless, but before I go there, let's jump to another subject matter real quick from our vocabulary.

Let's take a moment to explore what it means to be business poor:

I don't believe there is a real definitive definition or answer, but I will share my experience and what it means to me. I put everything, I mean everything, into my businesses; it was my life. My business was my life and my everything. It's all I talked about, thought about and it was almost all I felt like I had. I didn't have a spouse, a significant other, nor pets. Of course, I had my family, my siblings and parents, but they were living their own lives with their own families pursuing their goals and raising their kids. So, I was doing me and doing me meant building a big business and giving back to the community through mentorship and leadership. It's just who I was, at least who I thought I was at the time. I was doing in my twenties what people said most people do in their forties. It was one of the most amazing feelings to bring so much income in that I could afford to hire a staff and make payroll so that they could provide for their families. I mean it was an amazing feeling. I was big stuff cutting checks and all and most entrepreneurs with big hopes and dreams have the same goals and aspirations because we know it's not just about us; it's about helping others and making a difference with our many talents and skills.

However, you can't keep giving from your cup. You must give from your overflow. Reread that if you didn't quite understand. I was giving from my cup; I didn't have my personal affairs in order. I was spending everything I earned to keep the business running. Let me be transparent. I was paying out over $2000 a month in bills at the salon, not including payroll and other expenses and barely spending $300 for my living expenses. This made me "business poor." I was so wrapped up in growing my business that I didn't care that I was homeless. I wasn't living on the street. I actually lived less than a 3 min drive from my business. I could walk in less than 10 minutes. It was literally around the corner. Convenience breeds contempt and boy was I content with immersing myself in my business and blocking out everything else.

Amidst all the excitement, I was informed that I would get tired. Me, being my young ambitious self, I didn't take heed to the warning. I have been homeless more times than I can count. But it never stopped me or my will to win. When it's in you; it's in you! However, it was time for me to have a home. A place for peace, rest and relaxation.

> *You, my dear, are going to get tired. Words I will never forget.*

I understand getting it out of the dirt, doing whatever it takes by any means necessary. But there comes a time in your life when you will be elevated to the next level and that next level could simply be self-care and maintaining a healthy work life balance, along with mental and physical health. Just like your vehicle needs maintenance so does your body and your mind. Being homeless definitely doesn't breed healthy habits. When you're in your own space, the home that you have decorated, you are free to create and really begin to enjoy life. Things just seem to flow for you because you're able to move around with ease. I operated in a place of lack and fear for five years and during those five years I was going through my transformation. Once I began to break down that wall brick by brick, I began to move from lack and fear to prosperity and abundance. Life just got better for me and I was available to receive the provision that was already prepared for my vision. Waking up to a flooded apartment and becoming homeless was a set up for a comeback. Perception can either allow you to win mentally or to lose emotionally. The choice is yours.

Lesson: The Definition of Homelessness
Your name is not on a lease or deed; you may be here now, but you won't be here forever if you take action and make the necessary adjustments to change your circumstances. You are moving in the right direction just by reading this book and others like it. Never give up.

Chapter 8
DO YOU DO LEADERSHIP TRAINING?

I have a gift and I'm going to share my gift with you, but you have to promise me that you're going to use it. The key only works if you put it in the door, turn it and push.

My Project Manager at the time brought this gift to my attention. She said you have a habit of asking the right question to the right person at the right time. That's the gift, now please use it to your advantage. I pondered on that for a moment and agreed. You will notice there is one constant in all the stories and they usually begin with a simple question. I acquired all my mentors, coaches and leadership by asking a simple question, none of which I thought about too hard. But I knew not to ask a direct question like how much money do you make. I mean, really, the only people that make money work at the mint. I was too smart to do something so immature. I knew that I had to ask thought provoking questions, but again, none of the questions I asked to said persons were premeditated. They just felt right. This particular question was asked late 2015 right after the flood. You know, the one I talked about that left me homeless again. Yeah, it was around that time.

SHE'S ALL OVER THE PLACE

After humbling myself and moving into a salon that was almost across the street from the building I rented for almost 5 years, I asked the right question to the right people per usual and they would soon become my mentors. I was basking in my latest accomplishment of losing 100lbs and going from a size 22 to a 10/12, so I was somewhere up there on cloud 9 maybe even 10. Not realizing that I turned all my attention from the hurt and shame wrapped up in guilt from feeling like a failure in business into fuel to accomplish my weight loss goal. That's what most people do after a trauma; they turn their attention elsewhere instead of focusing on healing and processing what just happened. I mean, I sent my rent check to my landlord and it didn't clear the bank. So, it was clear to me that it was time to end that chapter and like I said, it was a hard chapter to end.

So, as I'm combing hair a client books an appointment with me and we all know that someone has to be the one to come try you out and if you're good, they will bring their whole tribe. Brothers, sisters, husband, cousin, friends and everyone they know. They will build you a whole clientele. Remember: word of mouth is the best form of marketing. After I did the first sweet baby, she asked could she bring her friend's daughter and of course I so sure, Ms. Precious loves the kids. They have their own bucket full of beads, bows and ribbons that they get to choose from before we begin their hair service. Me and my little sweet baby connected from the first time I did her hair. It was the cutest thing ever when her mother said my baby said she loves you, I asked her why and she said because she's weird. Her mother said, "What do you mean weird?" "She wears two different color socks like me." I was tickled pink. I know she felt my smile through the phone because I was cheesing, as we say, when someone is smiling so hard until their face hurts. She became my kid sister almost instantly and she was the only girl, so it was fitting. Her parents traveled a great deal to conferences and trainings, so I didn't see them often at first. However, when I did see them, I observed they drove luxury automobiles, not cars, but automobiles. If you know me you know that leadership training is a must, so I would go to some sort of training every year. After scheduling the kid sister's hair appointment, I asked her mom did she and her husband do leadership training? She said, "Excuse me, do you even know what we do?" I answered no ma'am. She said, "Well what made you ask me that question?" Well, every year I take at least one leadership training and I know you all travel a great deal for conferences and if leadership training was something you do, I would like to attend. I can tell she was a little taken aback because people don't usually randomly ask if you do leadership training, especially if they don't know what you do for a living. Her response was that it's a leadership company. I'm going to ask my husband if he will sit down with you and share what we do. He is really busy, but I will ask him and I said yes ma'am. A short time later, we were all sitting down at the private business club that we were both members of, but had never crossed paths.

See, when you're a little kid, people will often ask what you want to be when you grow up? We have all been asked this question. We would name all kinds of careers when we were kids. You're probably thinking to yourself now about all the things you wanted to be as a child. Well, when you grow up, the question then becomes what kind of life do you want to live? That's what he asked me after first asking me how much money I wanted to earn a month. Sitting in the tallest building in the state of South Carolina, which is 25 floors, I sat across from him in my size 10 dress. Remember, I had just lost 100lbs and I was feeling myself. I was attractive and I don't mean in a cute way. I mean that when you find someone that has accomplished something that the average person thinks is hard or impossible, it makes that person look attractive. They may just have the type of qualities worthy of your time. I had also kind of unconsciously felt like I had arrived thinking this weight loss thing was a destination instead of a journey. So my all over the placeness was searching for the next thing, the next opportunity to help this failure get back on her feet. My fear of failing in the first 2 years caused me to make some poor business decisions and cost me about $30k worth of debt. My answer to his question, which was how much money do you want to earn a month, was really simple for me at this point in my life. I answered $5,000 a month. I know that an extra $5k a month would help me dig my way out of the hole I dug. The look on his face was priceless, as if I had offended him in some way. So, after he shared his thoughts on my answer to his question, I readjusted my seat, leaned in with my fingers crossed in my hands, looked him in his eyes and said, "Well, I have earned six figures and that's $8,333.33 a month. But right now, $5k a month will help pay this $30k worth of debt I accumulated growing my printing company too fast." I continued with I know I'm going to be a millionaire, speak on platforms around the country and then around the world. He said, "Why stop at a million; go for the billion," and another seed was planted.

Ivan then smiled and proceeded to share with me who he was, what he did and what was in it for me. I was blown away by what I had learned about the financial services industry during our meeting. Some would say my nose was wide open. I wanted to learn more and I wanted to share what I learned with others. The more you share what you learn the more you retain said information. However, I was gearing up for a trip, I'm sorry, a vacation, to Hawaii for 10 days where I had some life changing decisions to make. After rewarding myself with a long-awaited sky diving excursion, I decided I would come back to South Carolina and see what I could learn from what would become another one of my greatest leadership and development mentors I have ever had. I was offered to manage several salons and barbershops on one of the most beautiful islands you can visit in Hawaii, but I turned it down and I'm thankful that I made the correct decision. Upon returning from my 10-day vacation, training would begin.

Over the next three years of my life, I was exposed to another world. It was one thing to read about the lifestyles of the rich and famous, but it was another thing to actually be submerged in it and get a taste of what life could really be like once you become financially independent. As all my other mentors, they took me under their wing, treated me like family and taught me so many valuable lessons. I built life lasting relationships. My Mr. Aaron, as I call him, always said if you save money one day money will save you. If you ask him what he does he will tell you all he does is ride, talk, and eat. Ivan Earle would always say that he is in the opportunity business. That was his 30-second elevator pitch.

When I was a little girl, I would see people driving nice cars and living in nice homes and I would say I wish I could just walk up to their door knock and ask them what they did to afford their lifestyle. I wasn't crazy enough to do it though, however my leadership question led me to the door. A door that exposed me to some of the greatest leadership training I had ever received and if it wasn't for me cutting my losses and staying positive about life, I would have missed out on so much. So, remember to get off that nail and stay out of your feelings. Ivan would say during his speeches that I have a PHD (public high school diploma) and I used it to get my MBA (my massive bank account)! Yep, that's where I got that from and I say it all the time. Thanks Ivan and Sharon Earle! There are no words that can describe the appreciation that I have for all that I learned about the financial services industry and about life as a whole. I'm forever grateful.

My overall principles and values were realigned because of that time in my life. I always told myself when you shed this weight and take care of yourself, your life is going to change. We focus so much on helping others that we neglect ourselves. Remember you give from your overflow not from your cup. If your hand is closed, no one can put anything in it and if it's all the way open, you can't hold on to anything. So, you must cup it a little. When you put God first, you will always win, at least that's what I believe. I learned that in life, it's God, family, education, then business. Principles I will live by forever. I learned how money works and what life insurance is really used for. Life insurance is income replacement. No one can replace a life, but you can replace their income. I learned how savings and investments work as well. Get exposed! Learning that minimum wage is $200k a year to a group of people was a game changer and a group of people that looked like me, made it all seem so real and it was.

Traveling for business or personal reasons and not having to spare any expense; truly having the best of the best. Being exposed to real leadership in such an environment was mind blowing. Going on vacation and enjoying your spouse or conducting business with ease because you travel with your nanny or child care provider. That way, you're not neglecting your family because your core values are God, family, education, then business in that order. Venting to your team because you only made $68k that month, then finding out later that a regular month is $100k will make you look at life, finances, and happiness differently. If you are the smartest or wealthiest person in the group, I suggest you get another group. You are the sum total of your friends. I've spent time with people who talked about becoming authors and earned a maximum of $6k a month until I learned the true meaning of that statement. It was time to get exposed and get a new circle. Now I didn't get rid of my friends and associates. I made new friends with higher incomes and people that were already authors, which exposed me to a new group of people. I visited and joined private business clubs. This not only allowed me to meet a new set of friends, but allowed me to experience another level of luxury and lifestyle. Remember you have to ask yourself what kind of life do you want to live?

> Learning how to have a threatening conversation in a non-threatening way was one of my greatest lessons and accomplishments. Thank you, Ivan Earle.

Lesson: What did you learn and what kind of life do you want to live?

Be thankful for every chapter of your life and always ask yourself what lesson did I learn from this and how can I apply it to my life right now. Ask yourself these questions often. What kind of life do I want to live? What lessons did you learn from your experiences and how are you applying them to your life?

Questions that changed my life and opened my eyes to another world of possibilities.

Jesus said unto him, If thou canst believe, all things are possible to him that believeth. Mark 9:23

Chapter 9
CAN WE GO TO LUNCH?

The titles of these chapters just keep getting better don't they? Yet again, another question that changed my life. You're always at the right place at the right time all the time. Yes, I was hungry; I'm always hungry, but that's not why I asked that question. It was almost time to break for lunch, but I wasn't thirsty. Metaphorically speaking, I'm always eager to learn from someone who has already done or is doing what I would like to do. Emulation is one of the best forms of flattery, especially if I want to do something you're doing and desire to learn from you. Thirsty meaning you jump into things without thinking twice, speaking and doing once. By this time, we have to not only pay attention to our surroundings, but we have to know how and when an opportunity presents itself and how to take advantage of it. So that's what I did; I seized an opportunity.

Ask yourself these questions:

Are you in the right room?

Asking the right questions?

With the right people?

CAN WE GO TO LUNCH?

All these can be life changing questions. If you would have told me that I would become really good friends with and become the personal assistant to Steve Harvey's Barber by asking him to lunch, I probably would have believed you lol. Just because I know how extra I am. "Extraordinary," that is, but it didn't quite happen that way. No one picked up the phone and told me that would happen. But that's exactly what happened. I didn't ask James "JT" Thomas, Steve Harvey's personal barber of 30 plus years, to have lunch just to share a meal. I asked him to lunch after he shared his story of how he became Steve Harvey's Barber because I knew he was hungry, but he wasn't thirsty. I believe that we could one day possibly have a mutually beneficial business relationship. I also know that real business men and women discuss business over a meal. Plus, we were breaking for lunch after he spoke, so I thought it fitting to ask him to lunch to secure a seat at his table.

I was sitting on the 1st row at the Atlanta Barber Conference in what some would call the hair capital of the world, Atlanta, GA, when I asked James to lunch. You couldn't miss me seeing as I had waist length braids that were pink, orange and yellow, a white top and skirt with a bright pink sweater that read in white print across the front "a lil bougie." I told you I have a knack for being unforgettable! My mom thought I had lost my mind wearing all those crazy hair colors in my hair. But we all go through our own little midlife crisis and I definitely was going through mine. I had hit rock bottom a few times over the past five years. The worst of the worst, prior to this conference, was the day I was in the salon servicing a client and my thumb literally slowly folded into my hand and kind of stopped working. I stopped and looked at my left thumb and I pulled it back out and it slowly folded into my hand again. I mean it scared the living daylights out of me. I immediately contacted my client before her and her daughter drove over an hour and a half to the salon. I knew I wouldn't be able to braid their hair and canceled the appointment. I held myself together and finished my client. I went to the doctor and paid out of pocket for a cortisone shot which was over $200 per shot. For the next few days to around a week, I sat in my mother's living room with my hands propped up with braces on both wrists, unable to work. It was one of the most miserable times of my life. I was homeless again because I decided to move in with my mother because my apartment had mold, which caused massive headaches. So, the complex let me out of my lease. I didn't see it then, but I was being set up for a come up seeing as my name wasn't on a lease. I had nothing to hold me back when I got the idea to go to the Atlanta Barber conference and not come back. I didn't have a job and I barely had $100 to my name.

After scrolling on Instagram in a depressed state, I started watching a guy named 10 stacks and the millionaire barber and learned of several conferences. I prepared as best as I could to go to the Atlanta Barber conference and decided what did I have to lose. Well, I didn't have much to lose, but while packing, I lost my wallet. I knew it had to be in the car and I had to find it seeing that the only cash I had was in the wallet. It was about $90, enough to get me to Atlanta and have a few bucks for food. I didn't plan on getting a room because my bestie, Jessica, lived there, plus I could always pull up to a planet fitness to take a shower if needed, which is what I had done in the past. I had no luck in finding my wallet, but my bank card and my license were in my pocket. You know the front chest pocket that all women have that isn't a pocket at all. Once I realized I couldn't find my wallet, I had an epiphany from the first book my mentor Mr. Gaddist gave to me when I was 21 years old. How to win friends and influence people. I remembered the part when he said if you need $100 and you only have 2 friends the probability is not that high, but if you have 10 friends your probability is higher of one of them helping you. So, I reached out to 15 people via text, phone, stopped by their office and I simply said, "I lost my wallet and I have to get to Atlanta for this conference. I'm not sure why, but I have to be there. Can you cash app me $15-$20 until Tuesday and I will pay you back? If you can't, I understand and thank you." As God is my witness, I had over $350 in my bank account in less than 3 hours. Not only did I make it to Atlanta for the conference, but I was able to book a room at the host hotel. Which meant I didn't have to sleep in my car at the hotel and go to planet fitness to take a shower. My best friend lived 45 minutes away and I was exhausted, so I didn't see myself making the drive.

Mr. Thomas shared with the audience that he told Steve no, not once, but twice when he offered him $500 a haircut then $1000 a haircut in the 80's. That was almost unheard of. Steve, at the time, was shooting his show in LA and wanted a barber that represented what he believed was his level of excellence and Mr. Thomas, being the barber and businessman that he was, fit the mold. Mr. Harvey finally offered him $1500 per hair cut twice a week, which was $3000 a week and to fly him to and from L.A. on Wednesdays and Thursdays, then he could fly home and still run his salons in Arlington, TX. He said you know what man, let me talk to my wife about it. He spoke to his wife and decided that he would give it a try. She said what do you have to lose?"

I was intrigued with the fact that not only was he humble and hungry, he was a risk taker. He took a calculated risk because he was hungry, not thirsty and didn't jump on the 1st offer. If he was thirsty, he would have taken the $500 or even the $1000. James worked with Steve for many years and they became great friends.

He was more than a barber and a friend. He was also Rickey Smiley's Road manager at one point. He produced movies, the Hoodie Awards and worked with countless celebrities. For me, I saw my next mentor standing in the front of the room. Someone who could not only teach me the basics to barbering, but someone that could help mentor me to the next level which is where I was ready to go. Someone who could assist in making my goals and dreams of impacting the beauty and barber industry a reality and he did just that. After creating M3, I said I would meet Steve Harvey and I did! In the spring of 2019, I was a volunteer barber at the boy's mentorship camp in Georgia, where I met not only Mr. Harvey, I even met Ne-Yo and took a picture with him.

> **Lesson:** When the student is ready, the teacher will appear! Sometimes this happens when you least expect it; just embrace it and go with it.

Chapter 10
THE LAUNDRY ROOM

How the hell did I end up here? Have you ever found yourself questioning yourself? I think we all have. I questioned myself and all the choices I had made in my short 36 years of life as I sat in the laundry room where I was currently living. How do you go from being a young successful entrepreneur, earning six figures, to being flat broke, unemployed, and overweight again? AND living in a damn laundry room no-less, I mean who does that!!!! I thought to myself. You do, I said out loud and you ended up here because you are exactly where you're supposed to be. You are at the right place at the right time all the time even if it is a damn laundry room.

We don't always understand the challenges we are faced with; however, you are exactly where your actions, reactions, and decisions have led you. I was listening to a motivational podcast episode on the way to the salon this morning. Chris Gardner, the first millionaire I told you I met, was speaking. As I listened to him, he addressed this very question and he answered: you drove here. He brought it to my attention and I will bring it to your attention as you may be asking yourself how in the hell did I get here wherever here is for you? He was homeless and in the Subway bathroom washing his son up and he looked at himself in the mirror and asked himself, "How did I get here?" I knew I wasn't the only person that talked to myself and answered. His response was quite profound. He said, "I drove." In other words, the answer to the question is you put yourself in whatever situation you're in and you have to be the one to take responsibility for getting yourself out. If you heard it once you have heard it 1000 times, "No one is coming to save you; you have to save yourself." Honestly, it wasn't until this exact moment as I type these words that I realized that I drove myself to that laundry room day in and day out for 9 months. You're probably wondering why I lived in a laundry room and whose laundry room I was living in, so I will share a little back story about this here laundry room.

When I decided to move to Texas, I knew it would be challenging (challenging also known as hard but I prefer to say challenging because everyone loves a challenge but most people won't do something that's hard). I knew little to no one in Texas, but being the professional best friend maker that I am, I had a few contacts in the DFW that I met the previous year when visiting for my niece's high school graduation. I jokingly said I may just move to Texas, not thinking or believing that it would ever really happen! But when I knew for sure I was going to relocate, I reached out and inquired about work and lodging. So, I knew I was going to be ok, plus I'm a survivor. I kept my gym membership at planet fitness so no matter where I was, I could always take a shower! I would sometimes fall asleep on the hydro beds and they would tell me you can't sleep here so I would get up and go to my car to finish off my nap. What I didn't know, however, was what the word commute meant when you live in Texas. But I learned real quick! When they say everything's bigger in Texas, they didn't lie.

I had no idea what it felt like to drive 30 minutes to work, let alone 45 minutes to an hour each way with traffic and please don't let it be raining or there be an accident. It felt like you would never make it home. I quickly discovered that I would need to work and live nearby without having to get on the interstate or any highway. For the first 6 months, I lived in Flower Mound, TX with friends of friends who were so gracious to rent me their spare bedroom for $100 a week. I worked in a warehouse through a temp agency that their friend worked for. Before this time in my life, you couldn't have paid me to believe I would have worked in a warehouse. I'm a hairdresser and a business owner. I was taught that the word JOB meant Just Over Broke. However, I came up with a new meaning. It became my Jesus Ordained Blessing. I had to cope and readjust to my new life. This chapter or season of my life was definitely challenging, but I embraced it. I had some serious lessons to learn about life and the biggest one was called HUMILITY. I was definitely in store for a ride.

I interviewed at several chain salons and hair cutteries, but I couldn't see myself signing up to make $8.00 an hour, so I told myself I would rather go to work in a warehouse than make $8 an hour cutting hair, plus I needed a change of scenery after doing hair for 15 years. However, I did consult with my praying best friend who helped me through so many of the storms I faced along my journey. It was the warehouse for me, long days and long nights, mandatory overtime, short breaks and even monitored bathroom breaks. As you can guess, I didn't last long in the warehouse world. I either quit or got fired even though I excelled quickly and was considered for a trainer position at one of the warehouses. I even got fired from one warehouse for talking! Can you believe that! I made several friends to whom I still associate with, some of which are now my hair clients.

It didn't take me long to decide to go ahead and operate in my passion and my gift, which is the amazing world of cosmetology and barbering. I was told in the height of my printing career to never forget that I'm a hair stylist by one of my clients' cousins. I had only met her that one time and she looked me directly in my eyes and said, "Don't you ever forget that you're a hairdresser" and it was kind of eerie like ok God, was that you because how could I forget when hair is my first love. I dismissed it at the time and kept on about my business of printing shirts and playing in people's hair because hair wasn't paying me what my printing business was at that time. I got so caught up in earning six figures and the idea of building the biggest printing company, that I lost sight of the big picture. It's not about you. Everything I went through up to this point is about YOU, yes, YOU reading/listening to this book.

Like the title of my book says, "She's All Over the Place," so let me take you down memory lane one more time before we get out of here. I will never forget the day a lady walked into my salon and asked me to do her daughter's hair and she even paid me in advance. I remember that day just as clear. I didn't believe depression was real until I met her daughter. She had suffered a major loss in her business and went from earning six figures to barely earning 2 figures a year. She ran a successful weight loss clinic and for some unforeseen turn of events, she lost it all and ended up working at a call center. She reminded me of that windup doll from the commercials for depression medicine. I mean she was miserable, sad, depressed, and lifeless. Her mother attempted to cheer her up with a fresh new hair style, which is how I came into the picture. We talked and I spread as much of my free motivation as I could in attempts to cheer her up as well. But I honestly didn't know if it was possible at that time. But time is the main Ingredient for healing. I remember saying a prayer for her and one for me too. I asked God that if I ever lost it all that He would allow me to see my way through. I assured Him that I would never lose my faith and that I would always put Him first. Just please, if I ever lost it all and got depressed, I desire to be able to come out of it and after 5 long years, here I am standing on the other side.

So back to living in the laundry room. Mr. Gaddist dropped a gem that I know I have repeated several times in this book and I will say it again. He told me there are some things in life you can't afford not to be able to afford. So, I knew I had to be resourceful and figure it out. After looking into renting a room at an Airbnb closer to the barber school that was in my price range, I found the laundry room. I was completing the cross over program with Mr. Thomas at his school Williams Barber College. Upon moving in, I was offered a discount on my rent to keep the house clean and to change the rooms when guests would check out. This allowed me to save even more money a month.

I dreamed of my luxury apartment home day in and day out with every amenity that I wanted as I laid in that laundry room at the Airbnb in Irving, TX where I lived for 9 months. We were in the height of the Pandemic and I had survival down to a science, but I was ready to live. My best friend said you are thriving, not just surviving. It was my therapist reminding me to create my budget, monies coming in and monies going out, along with desiring my own living quarters that pushed me to take action on bringing my goal of living in a luxury apartment home a reality. I got everything I wanted in my apartment with a bonus fireplace as stated where a 18x24 custom framed photo of myself hangs. I told my friends I felt like a real adult since I had a large portrait of myself above my fireplace. Sometimes it's the little things.

I was also a radio personality briefly on the James Thomas radio show before the Pandemic where we talked about all things hair! My segment was called, "How it is Done" and I shared with our listeners and viewers how to get the job done! I tell everyone I have a PHD, a Public High School Diploma and I'm using it to get my MBA which is my Massive Bank Account! There were several guests that stood out to me so I made sure to connect with them after the show, which is how I was able to find, in my opinion, the world's best PR agent and the salon suites that I eventually moved into to begin my career as a master hair care barber stylist in the DFW Metroplex. I signed a 3-year lease in the Arlington and Mansfield Texas area and I love it.

Once I completed barber school and found a salon suite, I was able to begin working on myself to process all that I had been through over the past five years. Being homeless on several occasions whether, it being due to a national disaster, mold or poor life choices. Being financially stable to barely having an income. I had to accept everything from my past business and life choices. I had made my bed and I had to lie in it and process it all, forgive myself and appreciate myself for all that I had accomplished. Learning how to heal was very challenging at first, but with the help of my amazing therapist, I can honestly say that I drank the prune juice and let that ish go!

We are so busy working towards the next big goal that we don't even realize that we have accomplished things that some people never will in their lifetime. Sitting in it allows you to really process and understand where you were, where you are and where you're going. I know all too well about being all over the place. Sometimes it can seem lonely, like no one understands you. Know that you are not alone. I suggest you seek out mentors, groups of like-minded people, coaches, advisors and a therapist. Your friends don't always have the answers or the correct treatment plan to help you cope with your past traumas. The types of therapy that I underwent were ACT (Acceptance Commitment Therapy) and IFS (Internal Family Systems). Those are the two I liked the most. Once I got out of my head, I began to see things clearly. Sometimes you can't see the buildings for the skyscrapers. The forest for the trees or the clouds for the sky.

So, get out of your head and go get some help, if not for you, for your family, friends and your future self. Remember, it's not about you. Your future's so bright you're going to have to wear shades, but you must get grounded and take care of your present self all while being mindful on your journey.

I will leave you with these questions: What kind of life do you want to live? What kind of life do you want to live? That wasn't a typo. I wanted you to ask yourself that question several times. One more time for good measure. What kind of life do you want to live? It doesn't matter how young or old you may be, this question applies to us all and is very important. If you don't know, then you will just drift through life with no aim or purpose.

> **Lesson:** Trust the process and learn how to be humble. Learning to have humility and integrity have proven to be, you guessed it, that right's right, life changing. Change your mind; change your life.

Peace I leave with you, my peace I give unto you: not as the world giveth, give I unto you. Let not your heart be troubled, neither let it be afraid. John 14:27

FINAL THOUGHTS

Well you made it to the end my dear friend. My hope is that as you orchestrate the symphony of your life, you would consider adding these suggestions to your day-to-day life. These suggestions are just that, suggestions. I learned a long time ago, you can't tell anyone what to do, not even a two-year old. So, I leave you with these suggestions so that when people tell you you're all over the place, you too can just smile because you know it just means you will be international someday. How about Wednesday because someday and one day aren't on the calendar!

These Suggestions are actions, thoughts, words and disciplines that will allow and assist you along your journey.

Suggestions
1. Pray to your higher power
2. Say thank you (attitude of gratitude)
3. Learn humility
4. Learn/ Practice Meditation
5. Acquire mentors
6. Read books
7. Relax
8. Write down your goals daily
9. Find a therapist
10. Go for a walk
11. Journal as frequently as you desire (don't forget to timestamp)
12. Use the smart goal setting system

13. Give back
14. Make new friends
15. Ask questions
16. Make exercise and healthy eating a lifestyle
17. Find work life balance
18. Take leadership courses
19. Travel
20. Slow down
21. Build mutually beneficial relationships
22. Support your peers
23. Listen to audio daily, even if it's just 15 minutes
24. Be kind to yourself and others
25. Take calculated risks
26. Tithe of your time, talent and finances
27. Forgive yourself
28. Network and barter to grow
29. Detach your emotions from your business
30. FAIL AS BIG AS YOU CAN!

I could go on, but I will save some for the next book. I appreciate you for taking the time to join me as I continue to embark on my journey to self-discovery. I hope my experiences give you not just a look into my failures, successes, and lessons, but that you decide to share your journey with the world. Your stories, our stories, help mold and shape the world. If she can do it, so can I. If he overcomes his obstacles, so can I. Always remember it's not about you. The sooner you let go, the sooner you will heal.

I'm so very proud of you and me. I'm excited about your future. It's so bright you're going to have to wear shades!

Have the best day ever, EVERYDAY! Love you mean it! It's ya girl Ms. Precious signing out!

Books that changed my life:

- What to Say When you Talk to Yourself – Shad Helmstetter
- Think and Grow Rich – Napoleon Hill
- Rich Dad Poor Dad – Robert T. Kiyosaki
- How to Win Friends and Influence People – Dale Carnegie
- Swim – Walter Bond
- The Happiness Trap – Russ Harris
- Atomic Habits – James Clear
- The Bible
- Know Can Do – Ken Blanchard/Paul J Meyer/Dick Ruhe
- The Slight Edge – Jeff Olson
- The One-Minute Millionaire – Robert G. Allen/Mark Victor Hansen
- Becoming a Millionaire God's Way – Dr. C. Thomas Anderson
- Battlefield of the Mind – Joyce Meyer
- Purpose Driven Life – Rick Warren
- Work like a Slave Think like a Master – Collis Temple III
- Millionaire Barber Stylist:
- How to Retire from Behind the Chair – Uchendi Nwani/Velma Demonbreun
- Steve Harvey's Barber...Says It All – James Thomas / Revonne Leach Johnson
- Leadership: Seeing and Seizing the Opportunity – Pastor Jeffrey James
- Pushing Up People – Art Williams
- Tax Journal – Kadenia Williams Javis
- Coach the AL Williams Story – Art Williams
- The Secret – Rhonda Byrne

CONCLUSION

Yes Yes or YES... it's time to tell your story. As we all know, "The struggle is real: real life topics" applies to us all. I always say that the things we go through are not about us at least that's what pulled me through the tough times. Sharing my story has not only liberated me, but has allowed me to show the world that you can overcome obstacles. Join me in the Motivate Me Movement known as M3 and choose your YES.

What do I mean by that? You can only say yes. You're either going to say yes right now, yes later are you gonna wish you would've said yes. So, which yes will you choose?

1st YES: You're saying yes right now and you're holding your camera over the QR code at the bottom of this page so you can get started on your journey to becoming an author in my next series, "The struggle is real: real life topics" so you can share your story.

2nd YES: You will pick this book back up a month or maybe a year from now or even 10 years and say YES, I'm ready to share my story and you're scanning the QR code to get started because you have now learned how real the struggle is and you really have a story to tell.

3rd YES: You take no action which means you've decided to sit around and wish you would have said YES to sharing your story with the world.

Which YES will you be?

CONCLUSION

You must do the following in this order:

Seed
Sow
Time
Work
Harvest

Made in the USA
Columbia, SC
18 January 2022